Royal College of Surgeons of England

The Reading of Words

A Study in Appreciation

Royal College of Surgeons of England

The Reading of Words
A Study in Appreciation

ISBN/EAN: 9783742820235

Manufactured in Europe, USA, Canada, Australia, Japa

Cover: Foto ©Andreas Hilbeck / pixelio.de

Manufactured and distributed by brebook publishing software
(www.brebook.com)

Royal College of Surgeons of England

The Reading of Words

A STUDY IN APPERCEPTION.

BY

WALTER BOWERS PILLSBURY, A. B., PH. D.,

Instructor in Psychology in Cornell University.

A thesis presented to the University Faculty of
the degree of Doctor of Phi

REPRINT FROM THE
AMERICAN JOURNAL OF PSYCHOLOGY, Vo
1897.

By WALTER BOWERS PILLSBURY, A. B., PH. D.,

Assistant in Psychology, Cornell University.

(*Reprint from the American Journal of Psychology, Vol. VIII, No. 3.*)

INTRODUCTION.

In the past history of psychology, almost as far back as the beginnings of modern philosophy, there has been much controversy as to whether the immediate datum of sense or some more general factor of mind plays the greater part in determining the nature of conscious processes. One side holds, to state it baldly, that we have in consciousness nothing but sensations, and associations which are directly conditioned by the nature and previous connections of sensations; the other that there are further subjective or mental states which have no small share in shaping consciousness. The two views are the psychological echo of the old philosophical war cries of 'innate ideas' and 'the mind a *tabula rasa*': a legacy of Hume's impressionism and the Kantian *a priori*. In recent psychologies we find this antithesis represented by the associationists on the one hand, and the apperceptionists on the other: the former deny, the latter affirm, the existence in mind of elements other than sensations and their connections.

In spite of numerous and spirited debates on the question, there has been no attempt made, so far as we can learn, to employ experiment for its solution; and only too often observation has been used both scantily and carelessly. Our purpose in this paper has been to state the results of experiments which bear directly on the point at issue, and give evidence that promises to be of value in its settlement. It was our intention in beginning the experiments to try and discover the relative importance of sensation, and the more general or remote factors—if such there were—which are at work in the very simple and familiar action of *reading a word*. Briefly stated, the method employed was the reduction of the intensity of objective factors to a minimum, and the examination of the subjective factors that remained. As the work progressed, we found that the relation between the directly given sensations and the more subjective factors as a whole was comparatively simple, and that the real complexity of the problem was bound up with the classical antithesis, within the subjective elements, between apperception and association. This has, therefore, received a very large share of our attention.

When we came to report the results, we found it very difficult to give accurate definitions of the terms that must be used to make clear the exact relations of the different concrete processes. The most convenient and the simplest way to do this, everything considered, was to follow some standard treatment of the subject, as a guide through the various complexes. We have, therefore, given a *résumé* of Wundt's theory of apperception and its relations to the other mental activities as an introduction to our own work. Wundt was chosen because he gives the most comprehensive and systematic discussion of the question, and is, moreover, one of the very few writers of scientific accuracy who have held the apperceptive view. It would, of course, be useless to discuss apperception upon the basis of a system which attained only negative results in this respect. We have constructed a connected exposition from the statements in the *Grundzüge der physiologischen Psychologie* (4th edn.), the "Lectures on Human and Animal Psychology," the *Logik* (2d edn.), the *Ethik* (2d edn.), the *System der Philosophie*, and the articles *Zur Lehre vom Willen* and *Bemerkungen zur Associationslehre*, published in the *Philosophische Studien*. We found that much has been made by critics of what seemed, on superficial examination, to be inconsistencies in Wundt's doctrine. Most of these disappear with a more complete knowledge of his works. Nevertheless, in one or two cases we believe that different conclusions can or must be drawn from the premisses which he has assumed. The theory as a whole is unaltered, and no material has been used in any part of the discussion except that furnished by Wundt himself. It is hoped that an impartial statement of Wundt's attitude towards this question will be of some value to the English-speaking student of psychology, even apart from the use we have made of it in connection with our own investigation.

We have found no literature that bears exactly on our more special problem. It is, of course, impossible in a paper of this scope to examine even superficially the more general literature of the subjects involved. We have, therefore, trusted to our *résumé* of Wundt and the very widespread knowledge of the theories of association to furnish the discussion with a historical setting, and to give a clear statement of the problems involved. Credit for suggestion of experimental methods has been given, where due, in the main body of the article.

CHAPTER I.

THE PSYCHOLOGY OF APPERCEPTION.

SECTION 1. APPERCEPTION AS CONSCIOUS PROCESS.

In discussions of apperception we must distinguish three uses of the word. Apperception may be used (1) to designate certain phenomena actually given in consciousness. (2) A second very general use is to denote a certain activity, whose existence we infer from these conscious data. Both meanings are perfectly valid in psychology. The immediate datum of consciousness may be either an actual element of conscious contents, or a certain change in that contents. Sensations we know directly. We also know, *e. g.*, that under certain circumstances sensations which have previously been in the mind return accompanied by peculiar states of mind which indicate that they have been in consciousness before. This knowledge forms the immediate datum of memory. But, in addition to this, we conceptualise the fact, or infer from it a general tendency of sensations to recur in consciousness. This, too, we call memory,—and with equal right. The same distinction holds true of apperception. The concept 'apperception' is not directly given in mind, any more than the concept 'memory'; both are immediate inferences from the actually given contents.

There are certain given phenomena of consciousness, which may be explained by the assumption of an apperceptive activity ; and we may use the concept to generalize the given, just as the physicist assumes ether to explain various phenomena of the physical universe. But further, in many cases, after the concept has been formed, it is used as if it stood for an immediately given, not an inferred process.

This use is legitimate as a short-hand expression for the whole procedure of observation and inference which led to the formation of the concept. But it cannot, of course, give any warrant for ascribing to apperception a substantial exist-ence. It still remains a convenient category under which we may group a number of related phenomena, but which itself has no existence in the sense that the phenomena them-selves are existent.

Besides these two legitimate psychological uses of the term apperception, there is (3) the varying and indefinite meta-physical use. This is in general related to the psychological uses from which it has developed. To trace the relation in detail would take us too far from the proper subject of this paper. It has, moreover, been thoroughly worked out by Dr. Staude. [1]

The first two uses of the word occur indiscriminately throughout Wundt's works. In nearly all cases the context gives a ready means of determining which of them is intended. In general, the concept apperception is meant in all passages except those concerned with an analysis of the immediately given. No confusion results if the distinction has once been noticed. On account of the great convenience of the double use, we shall follow Wundt in adopting it.

Wundt declares that his ' apperception ' is not a metaphys-ical concept, not the addition of a new faculty to mind. Ap-perception stands simply for a certain group of conscious phenomena, which have such definite relations, and so many marks in common to distinguish them from the other mental contents, that they deserve a special name. In beginning a discussion of Wundt's doctrine, we must, therefore, deter-mine exactly what processes he includes under the term.

As we observe our ideas, we find that some are distinct and clear, while others are vague and indefinite. In this dif-ference in degree of clearness Wundt finds the first and most prominent of the facts to which he applies the name apper-ception, and about it he groups the other phenomena to be included under the term. This difference is not a difference in the ideas themselves, as contents, but a mere changing ac-cident of their appearance in consciousness. The clearest ideas may become vague, while the vague ideas of the con-scious background may grow clearer, and assume a promi-nent place. The change is best illustrated by Wundt's met-aphor of *Blickpunkt* and *Blickfeld*. At any given moment we have certain portions of the ' field of consciousness ' at the ' point of clearest vision.' From this clearest point, the

---

[1] *Phil. Studien*, I, pp. 149 ff.

ideas shade off in all degrees of clearness down to the greatest obscurity. But the relations of the ideas to each other in degree of clearness are not fixed. The point of clearest mental vision *(innerer Blickpunkt)* may move over the entire range of consciousness, just as we may move the *fovea* of the eye over the entire field of vision, and bring each point into the place most favorable for its seeing.

Difference in clearness is not the same with difference in the intensity of the idea or sensation, though it may in part be dependent upon intensity. This is best seen in the variations of very weak stimuli. Here we can easily distinguish a variation in the degree of subjective clearness from a change in the objective intensity of the sensation. A little care in observation, however, serves to make the difference apparent even in sensations of average intensity. In extreme cases, when the stimuli are very near the limen of sensitivity, we may have sensations which lie above the intensity limen, but below the limen of clearness or apperception. | Ideas may be below the apperception limen and still be in consciousness. The general relation of intensity to clearness seems to be reciprocal. Intensity favors clearness, clearness favors intensity. The increase of intensity accompanying or following increase in clearness is induced only indirectly by apperception. It depends directly upon the motor discharges called up by association during apperception.

That difference in clearness is not a function of single ideas and not occasioned by the external stimuli to ideas or sensations, is shown by the fact that degree of clearness varies with the number of ideas contained in the *Blickpunkt* at a given time. If one idea alone occupies the important place in consciousness, it is much clearer than if several others are equally prominent. In Wundt's terminology, the clearness of the apperceived ideas varies inversely with the number of ideas simultaneously apperceived. This interrelation between the number of ideas and their degree of clearness seems to indicate that we are dealing in apperception with a factor which is of wider influence than any single idea.

Preceding, accompanying and succeeding increase in the clearness of ideas there is a varying complex of sensational and affective phenomena which deserves very close description and analysis. It appears most simply in the processes accompanying the immediate arousal of a sensation through the sense organ. Here Wundt[1] makes it consist of four elements: (1) increase of clearness in the idea directly before the mind, accompanied by the immediate feeling of activity

---

[1] *Phys. Psy.*, II, pp. 274 f.

(Thätigkeitsgefühl) ; (2) inhibition of other ideas; (3) muscular strain sensations, with the feelings connected with them, intensifying the primary feeling of activity; and (4) the reflex effect of these strain sensations, intensifying the idea apperceived. Of these four elements which Wundt distinguishes we can regard only the increase of clearness (which we have discussed above), the feeling of activity, the strain sensations with the increase in the feeling of activity which accompanies them, and probably the increase in intensity succeeding the strain sensations, as directly given in consciousness. The immediately inferred constituents are the inhibition effects, and the dependence of the increase in intensity upon muscular excitations. The conscious facts in these two cases are that other ideas do not come to consciousness, or to the clearest consciousness, while we are attending to some given idea, and that the entering ideas grow in intensity after the strain sensations appear. We shall find it necessary later to question how far the feeling of activity is elementary, and how far analysable into simpler elements.

Besides the direct accompaniments of apperception in attention, there are others, more remotely related, which often precede and accompany them. These again always seem, when analysed, to consist of strain sensations, of more or less dark ideas, and of the affective tone which the process produces. They are very marked in expectation and the succeeding state of satisfaction or surprise.

In expectation Wundt distinguishes three important factors : oscillation between the ideas of the various objects expected; sensations of strain,—especially from the muscles of adaptation in the organ from which the sensation is expected ; and feelings (for the most part, evidently, the sense feelings of pleasure-pain) which arise partly from the strain sensations, and partly from the unrest due to the vibrating memory images. With the entrance of the expected idea we have the state of satisfaction *(Erfüllung)*. Here we find a feeling of passivity, followed by a feeling of activity and the feeling connected with normal adaptation. Should an idea enter which was not expected, we have surprise. Here the feeling of passivity lasts for a longer time; the feeling of activity enters but slowly ; and the accompanying feeling of disagreement with the expected idea gives the whole process an unpleasant affective tone. In both these complexes, therefore, Wundt sees, ultimately, nothing more than increase in clearness of sensation, a changing affective tone, various strain sensations, and ideas that come and go in the dark background of consciousness.

There are two strong pieces of evidence, he says, that the

phenomena of this group are causally related. (1) They always occur together in time. An idea never undergoes the peculiar increase in clearness when the accompanying phenomena mentioned are not present. This is definitely stated by Wundt[1] as follows : "Careful introspection seems to show that feelings of the same kind are never entirely absent, where ideas which were formerly obscure become clearer, although their intensity be much less and their quality exceedingly variable." (2) The feeling of activity and the sensations of strain are most intensive when the ideas are clearest. Increase in clearness of ideas and in intensity of strain sensations, etc., always go on side by side.—Thus two of Mill's canons of induction apply to the case under discussion, and the evidence that there is some fundamental relation between the two processes seems very strong, if it is not indeed conclusive.[2]

So far all has been plain sailing. We have discovered that sensations change in a way which seems to be independent of the individual sensation, and of the objective causes of sensation in general. We have three decisive bits of evidence that this change is peculiar, and only partially dependent upon the ordinary attributes of sensation. Unlike them, it is almost entirely independent of the objective conditions of sensation. (1) It is not like quality, or extent, and other attributes of sensation, dependent merely upon the character of the stimulus. Changes in clearness take place while all external conditions remain the same. Dark or confused sensations increase in clearness ; the clearer sensations at one moment become the confused at the next, without reference to changes in the external world. (2) Although a reciprocal relation exists between clearness and intensity (the attribute to which it is most similar), the two are different and distinguishable. They are independent variables. A sensation of

---

[1] "Lectures," p. 248.

[2] The word 'feeling' is used, here as elsewhere, by Wundt in a peculiar sense, which must be made plain if we are to understand much of his discussion. A 'feeling' is a reaction of the total organism upon any phenomenon. As a conscious process it is a characteristic mark of the presence of the phenomena which occasion it, and is usually regarded as simple and unanalysable. Nearly every feeling has its opposite : pleasure and pain are opposed, as are the feeling of activity and the feeling of passivity. But, as we shall see later, there are some feelings (e. g., the conceptual feeling:cf. p. 337 f.) which do not stand in any such antithetical relation to others. It should be noticed, in particular, that 'feeling' (Gefühl) does not always refer to feelings of pleasantness and unpleasantness. We have sometimes used the word 'affection' or 'affective tone' in place of feeling in this restricted sense.

small intensity may be very clear, while a comparatively very intensive sensation may hardly affect consciousness at all, may remain dark and confused in the conscious background. (3) That clearness is not a function of any single sensation is apparent from the inverse ratio between degree of clearness and the number of clear ideas,—between the extent and intensity of the *Blickpunkt*. Were clearness a function of the individual sensation, it would not be affected by the variation of another sensation in the same respect. This very involved relation between the variations of different sensations under certain conditions seems to preclude the possibility that the attribute thus affected is dependent merely upon the sensation to which it attaches for the moment. The three sets of facts, then, seem to render it very improbable that we are dealing with a phenomenon of consciousness which is dependent upon a single sensation or upon external conditions.

If this phenomenon stood alone, it would of itself be sufficiently important to deserve notice. It becomes still more striking when we consider the importance of the phenomena which accompany it. The strain sensations, the affective processes, and the cloud of darker ideas scattered about the focus of consciousness, before and during its occurrence, constitute a group respecting which we cannot but be of Wundt's opinion, that it is worthy of special description and a special name.

The number and nature of the elements in the complex of concomitant processes are in general clear enough from the analysis of attention and expectation which has been summarised above. The complex consists of numerous strain sensations, and a general affective tone, which is excited partly by these strain sensations and partly by the sensations which take part in the process.

So much of the description is completely unambiguous. Here and there throughout the different discussions, however, we meet with a mention of a feeling of activity *(Thätigkeitsgefühl)*. It is not immediately evident whether by this is meant something ultimate and unanalysable, a direct consciousness of an element of mind different from sensation or pleasure-pain, of apperception in what we have called the concept sense of the word ; or whether it is merely a convenient term used to designate a complex of affection and sensations from which we naturally and directly infer that an activity has been at work. We are told repeatedly that we can know apperception only by its effects upon sensation and feeling; but the implication of many of the discussions is that we know it immediately, in the *Thätigkeitsgefühl*. We must decide in favor of one view or the other from a careful examination of the various passages in Wundt's works in which the question is discussed.

Two kinds of evidence are available in this connection. We can examine analyses of the apperceptive process, for evidence of identity or non-identity of the *Thätigkeitsgefühl* with the sensational and affective contents usually mentioned as present ; and we may look for and evaluate passages that state explicitly that apperception appears in consciousness immediately. One of the passages which offers the most unequivocal evidence of the former kind is in the *Zur Lehre vom Willen*. After analysing the side-contents of consciousness during the apperception of an idea into feelings and innervation sensations, Wundt says: "In diesen Innervations-empfindungen liegt zugleich der nächste sinnliche Anlass dafür, dass wir die Apperception oder Aufmerksamkeit eine Thätigkeit nennen und sie als solche von dem völligen passiven Verhalten gegenüber äusseren Eindrücken oder in uns aufsteigenden Vorstellungen unterscheiden."[1] Lower down on the same page he gives an equally decisive analysis of will and apperception to prove that they are the same. "In der That sind bei derselben [die primitive Willens-handlung = die Apperception] die bei jeder Willensthätig-keit zu unterscheidenden Stadien auzutreffen : die Erregung des Bewusstseins durch ein Gefühlsmotiv, die daraus hervorgehende Richtung des Bewusstseins mit ihren psy-chischen und physischen Folgezuständen, und endlich die durch die letzteren herbeigeführte Lösung der Spannung."

Similarly the analysis of expectation,[2] which Wundt calls the apperception of a future, not a present idea, is reduced entirely to strain sensations, to affective states accompany-ing the strain sensations, and to the oscillation of the dark ideas in consciousness. So in the "Lectures"[3]: "The whole circle of subjective processes connected with appercep-tion we call *attention*. Attention contains three essential constituents : an increased clearness of ideas ; muscle sensa-tions, which generally belong to the same modality as the ideas ; and the feelings which precede and accompany the ideational change." Thus wherever Wundt gives an exact analysis of the processes which he includes under the *Thätig-keitsgefühl*, he seems to reduce it mainly to sensations of strain or (as in the older article cited) of innervation. The 'sensations of innervation' are, of course, equivalent to the 'strain sensation' of his modern work. This is evident from

[1] *Phil. Stud.*, I, p. 347.
[2] *Phys. Psy.*, II, p. 280.
[3] P. 249.

the general change of terms between older and newer editions. It is seen more particularly in the present connection from the fact that the sensations of innervation reflexly increase the intensity of the sensation, — a function which is ascribed in the fourth edition of the *Physiologische Psychologie*[1] to strain sensations.

The direct statements concerning the conscious phenomena of apperception or, as Wundt usually states the problem from the other point of view, of the way in which apperception comes to consciousness, seem just as definite in favor of the same interpretation. Thus in the *Physiologische Psychologie*, II, p. 279, after speaking of the relation of passive and active apperception to association, Wundt says, "In beiden Fällen kommt uns aber als ein von dem Verlauf der Vorstellungen verschiedener Vorgang die Apperception theils durch die sie begleitenden Gefühle, theils durch die begleitenden Spannungsempfindungen zum Bewusstsein, deren Intensität mit dem Grad der Aufmerksamkeit zunimmt."

Yet stronger are the statements in the fine print at the end of the same chapter,[2] in which he defends himself from the charge of introducing metaphysical concepts into psychology.

"Metaphysische Begriffe bezeichnen nicht Thatsachen sondern speculative Ergänzungen derselben. . . . . Dagegen verstehe ich hier wie überall unter Apperception lediglich die sämmtlichen oben geschilderten einfachen Phänomene selbst: die Veränderungen im Klarheitsgrad der Vorstellungen, die begleitenden Gefühle, die mir, je nachdem das Thätigkeitsgefühl das ursprüngliche ist oder das Gefühl des Erleidens ihm vorausgeht, zugleich das nächste Unterscheidungsmerkmal der activen und der passiven Apperception abgeben, endlich die begleitenden Spannungsempfindungen und, wo sie vorkommt, die an die letzeren gebundene schwache Verstärkung der in ihrem Klarheitsgrad gehobenen Empfindungen. Natürlich bin ich nicht der Meinung, jene Gefühle der Thätigkeit und des Erleidens enthielten an und für sich irgend etwas von den Vorstellungen oder gar den Begriffen, die wir mit diesen Ausdrücken verbinden; vielmehr liegt hier genau der nämliche Fall vor, wie bei den elementaren Empfindungen: ihre Namen müssen wir gewissen Vorstellungsbeziehungen derselben entnehmen, ohne dass damit jemals gemeint sein kann, diese Vorstellungen selbst seien in ihnen enthalten."

This passage appears to indicate not only that Apperception is primarily merely the name for a group of conscious phenomena, but that the peculiar *Thätigkeitsgefühl* is itself but a complex of other feelings, which we frequently meet, and that its peculiarity is due to peculiarity in the combination of familiar sensations and feelings rather than to any

[1] II, p. 274.
[2] *Ibid.*, II, p. 283.

new mental element. Still further support for the same view is given by a sentence at the bottom of the page quoted: "Ebenso scheint es mir, dass der Versuch die Vorgänge der Apperception und der Aufmerksamkeit in die Elemente zu zerlegen, die den überall sonst uns begegnenden Elementen des seelischen Geschehens entsprechen, das Gegentheil von dem ist was man die Construction eines neuen Seelenvermögens nennen könnte." This is the general tenor of all Wundt's statements which give us a direct account of the precise way in which we are conscious of apperception. It seems to reduce to a complex of changes which appear in consciousness when the favored idea increases in clearness. The feeling of activity covers the most striking part of this complex, the part which is most prominent in the 'spontaneous' acts of mind.

That an activity is to be inferred from certain states of consciousness is, then, the meaning of the passages so far. The phenomena from which activity is inferred are now grouped together under the name of *Thätigkeitsgefühl*, and under the conceptualising tendency to which we called attention at the beginning of the chapter, activity or spontaneity is referred to as if it were an element of which we were directly conscious. In the passages we have considered, Wundt is thus analysing and grouping the phenomena which permit the inference that there has been activity, and so justify him in giving these a distinct name. A passage in the same connection as those quoted above from the "Zur Lehre vom Willen"[1] seems to show that this procedure has been followed consciously.

"Ich gebe zu, dass in der hier gegebenen Schilderung gewisse Elemente mehr aus Folgeerscheinungen erschlossen als direct beobachtet sind. Immerhin wird der Versuch gemacht den in der gewöhnlichen Vorstellung völlig unbestimmt gelassenen Begriff der 'spontanen Thätigkeit' so viel als möglich in seine Elemente zu zerlegen und darüber Rechenschaft zu geben, warum wir gewisse Vorgänge auf eine innere Thätigkeit beziehen und andere nicht."

If we have correctly interpreted Wundt's statement of the conscious effects of apperception, it is nevertheless easy to see how he would speak of the immediate consciousness of a *Thätigkeitsgefühl* as he does, and assume that the reader would refer to the explanatory passages for the exact meaning of the term. The concept is used for convenience in place of naming the separate elements in each case. Our explanation is further supported by the fact that the passages which

---

[1] *Phil. Stud.*, I, p. 347.

can be interpreted to imply an immediate consciousness of a peculiar *Thätigkeitsgefühl* are either (1) introductory passages,[1] where it is particularly desirable to emphasise the distinctions between this complex and others more or less similar to it, or (2) passages in which the process is mentioned only incidentally. Still a third connection in which the word is used in the same general significance occurs in the *Ethik* (pp. 435 f., *e. g.*), where the point in contention is that voluntary action is conscious and is not merely inferred from the phenomena of external movement. Here, then, *Thätigkeitsgefühl* is a descriptive term, indicating that there are some conscious processes which accompany voluntary action, but not implying anything as to the nature of these processes.

SECTION 2.   PASSIVE AND ACTIVE APPERCEPTION.

The group of processes which has for its core the increase in degree of clearness of some idea, seems to be of two general kinds, which Wundt denotes by the terms 'passive' and 'active' apperception. The ground of this classification is furnished mainly by the quality and intensity of the concomitant strain sensations and feelings. Active apperception is accompanied by the *Thätigkeitsgefühl*, which we have discussed at length in the preceding Section; passive apperception by a feeling of passivity. The difference is almost entirely one of intensity in the concomitant phenomena.

Passive apperception appears to have two forms, or, rather, to be present on two occasions, one of them independent of, the other closely connected with, active apperception. (1) At certain times when an idea enters consciousness under the most favorable conditions, we have only passive apperception; while (2) in other cases passive apperception takes place first, and is succeeded by active. In neither event is passive apperception so complete or full as direct active apperception. There is a feeling of being at a loss, of insufficiency—as in the emotion of surprise—which hinders the proper or usual increase in degree of clearness. The strain sensations are fewer in number and less intensive, and the idea does not become so clear. Or, as Wundt sums up the description himself[2]: "Demnach unterscheidet sich objectiv die passive von der activen Apperception lediglich durch den geringeren Klarheitsgrad der Vorstellungen, durch die völlig mangelnden oder nur spurweisen und rasch verge-

_____

[1] *Phys. Psy.*, II, p. 266.
[2] *Phys. Psy.*, II, p. 277.

henden Symptome motorischer Innervation und der von dieser ausgehenden associativen Verstärkung der Empfindungen.''

Another accurate and detailed analysis of this complex of sensations is given in the " Lectures " (p. 254). " Even passive apperception, therefore, has its attendant feelings[1]; only that these are associated to form a total feeling with a character of its own, either exclusively conditioned by the quality and intensity of the ideas that happen to be present in consciousness, or (and this is especially the case in apperception of very intensive external sense-impressions) consisting in a feeling of inhibition, which appears to arise from the sudden arrest of existing tendencies in the formation of ideas.'' Here we see that the feeling of passivity is not entirely unanalysable, any more than the feeling of activity. It seems also to be like the latter in its components, and is in the main but another species of the same genus.

A better distinction between passive and active apperception depends upon the cause in the two cases, or, to speak in concrete terms, upon the states of mind which precede the apperception. In the typically passive form, apperception is determined unequivocally and immediately. There is no choice between several possible ways in which an idea may come to consciousness, or hesitation as to which of several ideas shall predominate in mind. One idea is so strong in interest or intensity that it overcomes all other applicants for the chief place in consciousness. In active apperception the incentives are more numerous and more evenly balanced. The decision is equivocal, and often delayed. Some time ordinarily elapses before we know which of the ideas that offer themselves will be chosen. In this hesitant decision, this trend of the incentives now towards the choice of one idea, now towards that of another, we see the most striking effects of the 'feeling of activity,' or as Wundt somewhat conceptually calls it in the *System*,[2] the 'feeling of self-activity.' The course of apperception is mainly determined by subjective causes, the individual characteristics of the mind, and its previous history.[3] These tend partially to conceal if not to counteract the effects of the external physical and physiological conditions which are most prominent in passive apperception. It is in passive apperception that we can best observe the effects of association, of the intensity of ideas and of the other chance or extraneous factors which

---

[1] For Wundt's general doctrine of feeling with particular reference to the *Totalgefühl*, see esp. " Lectures," p. 220.

[2] *System*, p. 567.

[3] *Phys. Psych.*, II, p. 576; *Logik*, I, p. 30.

have a determining influence upon the course of consciousness.

The distinction between passive and active apperception in terms of cause leads us to a discussion of the conditions and causes of apperception in general. The conditions of apperception fall into two classes, subjective and objective. The objective conditions are intensity[1] and frequency of occurrence.[2] The more often we have had a sensation, the more readily do we apperceive it. Moderate intensities favor apperception; weak sensations are not easily noticed, and the organism cannot adapt itself to very intensive stimulation.[3]

Subjective conditions may be best treated under two general heads : the conscious states immediately preceding apperception, and the entire disposition of the individual consciousness as determined by its previous history.[4] Of the first class the most important seem to be the memory images and externally aroused sensations which are present just before and during the total process of apperception. Apperception of any sensation is rendered easy by its separate and isolated appearance shortly before in consciousness. That it shall at some previous time have entered consciousness alone is a *conditio sine qua non* for apperception, when it appears in a complex of sensations, or at the same time with other sensations. This rule is illustrated by the ease with which we hear out an overtone, if we have heard its quality singly, just before the complex note has been struck.[5] In many cases a memory image does duty for the externally aroused sensation in facilitating apperception. This is strikingly illustrated by the ease and rapidity with which we apperceive an expected as compared with an unexpected idea. This difference really reduces mainly to the absence or presence of memory ideas.[6]

Of the less immediate conditions of apperception we have frequent discussion throughout Wundt's works. In considering them we have, of course, to deal less with what is immediately conscious at the moment of apperception, and more with the hypothetical and inferred. The general disposition of consciousness here plays the most important part. It finds a physiological explanation in the habits of the organism, which have been acquired partly during the history

---

[1] Intensity of course is partly due to proper adaptation of the sense organ.

[2] *Phys. Psych.*, II, p. 270.

[3] *Ibid.*, II, p. 271.

[4] *Logik*, I, p. 31.

[6] *Phys. Psych.*, II, p. 270. *Ibid.*, II, p. 280.

of the race, and partly in the life of the individual.[1] Where the sensational and associative factors which tend to determine apperception are fairly evenly balanced, this disposition decides in favor of one idea or the other. Its power is by no means inconsiderable, as can be seen from its activity in directing the attention upon weak stimuli when much stronger are present.

SECTION 3. APPERCEPTION AND ASSOCIATION.

Another important point in Wundt's theory of apperception is the way in which he relates it to association. In the previous Sections it has been shown that no sensation comes to its full rights in consciousness unless apperceived. Apperception either operates *actively*, as an arbiter between various sensations which seek to enter ; or must at least *passively* consent to the entrance of an idea which comes alone, or with strength or interest sufficient to win from its rivals without contest. 'Association' performs the same office for a recurrent sensation as the physical factors which first brought it to consciousness. Just as physical forces furnish us with original sensations, material for apperception, so the physiological factors which underlie association offer consciousness the crude material from which apperception must choose those elements which are to be worked up into the finished mental product.[2] Association, that is, gives the possible connections of ideas, from which apperception chooses those that are to become actual. Associatively, the idea a may at any time call up b, c, d, etc.,—but apperception decides that of these c alone shall actually arise.

So far as it is conscious, apperception consists here of the presence of one idea under conditions which have at other times given rise to other ideas. At times, again, we are conscious of dark, *i. e.*, only partially apperceived ideas, while a particular idea rises to clear consciousness, although all seem to owe their origin to their connection with one and the same primary idea. Successive apperception and rejection of ideas belonging to a single group furnish evidence of similar tenor. The choice is accompanied by the feelings and secondary sensations which we know in attention to external objects as the feeling of activity. The facts of choice, of the increase in clearness of one of several ideas, and of the familiar feeling of activity, are amply sufficient to mark off the apperceptive complex from the associative.

---

[1] *System*, p. 566; *Logik*, I, p. 30; "Lectures," p. 252; *Ethik*, p. 439; *Phys. Psych.*, II, p. 279.

[2] *Phys. Psych.*, II, p. 279; *Logik*, I, pp. 28, 31, 48 f.; *System*, pp. 565 f.

Here again we have to distinguish between the functions of passive and of active apperception. It is through passive apperception that we are able to recognise the effects of association. At this stage what we have termed the objective causes of apperception play the most important part. That is, the physiological processes which underlie association are unambiguous, and consequently give the selective agency no choice. There is but a single course for the train of ideas to take, and idea follows idea in the natural unrestrained order that physiological causes and earlier relations of sensible processes in the external world dictate. We are in presence of the true causality of associative laws.

In active apperception, on the other hand, the merely physiological causes, the external relations, take a subordinate place. The particular conditions of the moment are subordinated to the more general conditions of consciousness. The subjective causes of apperception are so strong that they conceal, to a greater or less degree, the more mechanical associations. Remote causes, that lie in the general nature and individual tendencies of consciousness, are predominant to determine which of the many possible ideas offered by association shall actually enter consciousness. Active and passive apperception thus designate the same processes as in the earlier case, where the raw material was furnished by external stimulus. In both instances, passive apperception is only the less prominent form of apperception : it is still apperception.

If this distinction is not carefully noted, the reader is liable to a misconception of Wundt's position in the first chapters of the *Logik*. There we often find associative connections opposed to apperceptive, and treated as if they were entirely distinct from the forms of apperception. It is not intended, however, to give the associative processes a concrete and independent existence in consciousness. The difference is one of degree, and of degree alone. In associative connections, the subjective causes of apperception play a much less important part than the objective ; in apperceptive connections the reverse is true, — subjective causes play the important rôle ; but in neither is one series of causes present alone. [1]

From this discussion it appears that the finished product, the concrete mental image, is always the apperceived idea. Association can be known only as we abstract from, or conceptualise, the process that goes on in our consciousness. We never know the *merely* associated material, any more

---

[1] *Logik*, I, pp. 28, 31, etc.; *System*, pp. 556 f.

than we know the immediate contribution of the senses. Both must be worked up by apperception before they become fully and clearly conscious. Neither pure sensation nor the product of mere association is directly given in consciousness. They must be inferred from the nature of the given, after it has been already apperceived. Conscious associative connections are, in other words, not merely associative connections, but connections with a minimal amount of apperception. [1]

The degree to which the subjective causes of apperception are effective in associative connections increases, in regular gradations, through associative synthesis, assimilation and successive association. The more detailed relations of these to each other and to the apperceptive connections, will be discussed in the next Chapter. It is sufficient in this context to call attention to the fact that the difference between all stages is one of degree alone, never of kind. [2]

The relation between apperception and association is reciprocal. Not only does association furnish apperception with the material upon which it acts, but the apperceived idea can reënter the associative train and become part of the material for a later apperception. After the idea has been apperceived, or several ideas have been united by apperception, the resultant idea enters into associative connections, and offers itself to apperception again in the natural course of mental phenomena. [3] Not only, then, are associated ideas apperceived, but apperceived ideas are associated. The two levels of consciousness are not distinct, but mutually interrelated.

CHAPTER II.

ASSOCIATIVE AND APPERCEPTIVE CONNECTIONS.

SECTION 1. ASSOCIATIVE CONNECTIONS.

We have seen in the preceding Chapter that Wundt finds in consciousness two general classes of connection. One is present in passive, the other in active apperception. One is mainly determined by the external and physiological conditions of the moment, the other by the more general conditions of the entire conscious disposition. The former class is that

---

[1] This view is opposed to Külpe's statement that association is not influenced by apperception. (Cf. *Die Lehre vom Willen in der neueren Psychologie. Phil. Stud.*, V, pp. 434 f.) Wundt's position in the *Logik*, however, is quite clear; and Külpe himself, in one passage, seems to incline to the opinion represented in the text.

[2] *Logik*, I, p. 31.

[3] *Logik*, I, pp. 50, 66; *System*, p. 566.

of associative, the latter that of apperceptive connections.

Wundt departs from ordinary usage in calling both the connections between ideas which are present in consciousness at the same time and those between ideas which succeed one another in consciousness, 'associations.' Indeed the difference between simultaneity and succession of ideas serves as the basis of his classification. Under each main head we have further several sub-classes, distinguished by the nature of the elements connected or by the closeness of the connection itself.

Simultaneous association takes three forms. We may have associations between sensations that enter consciousness together within the same modality, 'associative synthesis'; we may have association of a newly entering sensation with ideas already present, 'assimilation'; and we may have associations between ideas from different modalities, 'complications.' The first and last of these are of no special interest for our immediate purpose. In associative synthesis the elements are closely knit together about some prominent member of the group, and their individuality is frequently lost in the whole. A musical clang affords the best instance of this kind of association. In the complication, the different elements may be completely distinct and individual. Here, too, the elements come from different modalities. Examples of such a union are the connection between the idea of a word and the movements of the larynx that accompany its utterance in speech, and the connection of visual and tactual elements in the formation of the idea of a thing.

Assimilation concerns us more directly. The term includes all the phenomena that accompany the entrance of a sensation into consciousness. It thus covers the process which Herbart termed 'apperception.' A sense impression does not enter the adult consciousness alone, but always in connection with other processes. The new element is connected with others, which have themselves previously been connected with elements similar to it ; and the whole thus formed appears in consciousness as a unit. Striking examples of assimilation are the overlooking of misprints in proof-reading, and the subjective completion of the rough daubs of stage scenery to a landscape, etc. Equally good, though less striking instances, are found in nearly every form of perception. When the process is carried a step farther, *i. e.*, when the associated elements outweigh the original in number and importance, or when the conscious connections do not correspond to the connections of the moment in the external world, we have 'illusion' instead of perception.

Assimilation is found on analysis to consist of an 'association of identity' between the entering element and some element or group of elements previously present in consciousness. There is further an association by contiguity, which completes or fills out gaps in the origin&l idea. If, *e. g.*, I read 'shocolate' as 'chocolate,' I get first an association of identity between the last letters of the word given and the corresponding letters of the word-idea 'chocolate,' and these, by contiguity, give the 'c' immediately and simultaneously.

From assimilation to *successive* association the passage is easy. In memory, the recurring ideational elements (the 'centrally excited sensations,' to use Külpe's phrase) which are brought up by physiological connections, and which are primarily a result of earlier relations of stimulation in the physical universe, must be worked up, as in simultaneous association. A memory image never comes back to us,—is never identical as a whole with its original,—but is always simultaneously associated to other ideas. And here, as before, we have the effects of two kinds of association, association by identity and association by contiguity. The latter is in the present case partially successive, partially simultaneous. We have a series of elements, which come by contiguity one after another; but each is in turn simultaneously associated by contiguity to many new processes, and one of these outlasts the remainder and gathers yet others about it. It is the persistence of one element in every two succeeding ideas which constitutes association by identity; it is the fact that an element in one couple of ideas is associated by contiguity with an element which is identical in the preceding or succeeding couple that gives us association by contiguity.

The successive association is, then, always of the same class.[1] We have no degrees of closeness enabling us to distinguish different kinds of association. That the connection is close enough to produce the succession, to cause one idea to follow another, is all that is essential. It is evident, therefore, that we can classify only by the nature of the assimilations which group about the central element, *i. e.*, by the relations between the simultaneous associations which arise successively; unless, indeed, we adopt a classification in terms of the various sense modalities. But this seems undesirable, since the simultaneous associations have already been made, when the successively associated sensation enters; and the successive association itself is no more than a second-

---

[1] Wundt's classification by logical categories, *e. g.*, coördination, subordination, etc., is couched in terms of relations in the external world, and not of mental connections as such.

ary working over of the products of the first connection.

Prominent among the simultaneous associations of successive elements is the process of *recognition*. This takes three forms, dependent upon the order of apperception of the accessory elements in the simultaneous association. When the accessory ideas which give rise to recognition, with its characteristic feeling, are apperceived before the entering idea, we have *mediate* recognition ; when they are not apperceived until later, we have *immediate* recognition ; and there is a third, - intermediate form, in which both are apperceived simultaneously.

SECTION 2.   APPERCEPTIVE CONNECTIONS.

Apperceptive connections of ideas follow much the same course as associative. They, too, are classified as simultaneous and successive, according as the elements appear together or succeed one another in consciousness. They differ from associative connections chiefly in the more perfect unity of the resulting process, and in the predominance of active apperception, *i. e.*, of the subjective factors in the apperception.

Simultaneous apperceptive connections are divided into three classes : agglutinations, apperceptive fusions or syntheses, and concepts. (1) Agglutination covers all cases in which the single elements unite to form a new individual whole, but are not themselves lost in the complex. They still retain their distinct individuality, though they become members of a more complex individual unit. The best examples are found in the subjective arrangement of beats in a rhythm, and in the formation of compound words like 'windmill' in English or *Heer-führer* in German, which obtain a new meaning as a whole, without alteration of form or significance of the components.

(2) In apperceptive synthesis we have a closer connection. The elements are so fused that the individual members of the group are lost in the whole. This stage is shown in the amalgamation of tense forms and pronouns with the root of a verb.

(3) When the fusion has become complete enough, and a large number of elements have been united, one element comes to predominate, and in a way to represent the whole. We then have a concept.

The word (usually the predominant element) represents the mass because it can successively associate with many single ideas which are logically subordinate to it. Thus we can have the word ' triangle ' associated successively to very many different forms of three-sided figures. The word can 'dissolve' into any of them, without making us feel that the concept has suffered material change. The representative idea of the concept is the nearest approach that we have in the concrete consciousness to an 'abstract' idea.

Successive apperceptive connections are similar to the preceding, except that the elements follow one another in time. The dividing line between successive and simultaneous apperception is not clear cut and definite. The same mental process may belong first to the one, then to the other class. This is shown again in the development of language. The general tendency in the formation of the verb, e. g., has been from many separate elements (root, pronoun, tense forms) to a single element, and then to a re-separation of the complex thus formed into its original elements. It is more than probable that the mental picture has in the same time undergone a change similar to that of the word. The stages which the idea passes through between the opposite forms of judgment in one word and in many, of simultaneous and successive apperceptive connection, are very gradual.

There are many degrees of complexity in the successive forms of apperceptive connection. The simplest is the *judgment*. This consists in the apperceptive connection of two processes, one or both of which may consist of elements which have already been simultaneously combined by apperception.[1] Several such connections are often connected into a whole of a higher order, in a train of thought.[2] There is theoretically no limit to the complexity of the various elements which unite to form any of the members of the train of thought, or the separate thought or judgment. But no matter how great the complexity, the persistent unity of apperception is seen in the fact that always and everywhere the connection is by couples. All the connections reduce on analysis to simple connections of two elements, of two couples of elements, of one element and a couple, or of complexes of couples. In the train of thought, e. g., we always have connections by pairs, i. e., by simple propositions. Only when the propositions have been established and their connections shown, it is possible for single elements to be picked out of different pairs and again connected. This is the basis of the syllogism.

Nor is this the only evidence of the unity of apperception to be found in apperceptive connections. As we have seen, trains of thought may arise not only from connections of ele-

[1] *Logik*, I, pp. 59 f.
[2] *Logik*, I, p. 67.

ments, but also from the division of a given whole. Judgments are subdivided into concepts as well as concepts
united into judgments. In every case, the division is by di-
chotomy. It is this feature which most closely distinguishes
successive apperceptive from successive associative connections. It is this fact, too, which renders consciousness a
single line instead of a series of diverging lines, as it would
be if, *e. g.*, every association were effective in calling up
ideas.

SECTION 3.   THE RELATION OF ASSOCIATIVE TO APPER-
CEPTIVE CONNECTIONS.

The question of the exact relation of associative to apperceptive connections is not an easy one. The line cannot
always be sharply drawn, nor is there any intrinsic mark,
any entirely new element of consciousness, which invariably
distinguishes the one from the other. The most we can do
is to note the general tendencies of the two forms, and so
determine the approximate position of the dividing line.

We shall avoid a frequent source of misapprehension in
Wundt's system if we begin the discussion with a statement
of the striking similarity, rather than of the difference
between the two types of connection. The fact is that there
is no real fundamental difference in the nature of the elements concerned in them. Both alike consist of associative
elements, which have been apperceived and brought into
connection with the whole of consciousness. Both alike, *i. e.*,
are partly determined by the objective, partly by the subjective conditions of consciousness. The whole question
turns upon the *proportion* in which the two determinants
enter, or, in other words, upon the relation between passive
and active apperception.[1] The line can therefore be drawn
no more closely here than it could in the earlier Section. (Ch.
1, § 2.) Indeed, it cannot be drawn *so* closely, because now
we have to classify concrete objects, to recognize general
distinctions in concrete experience, instead of merely to
describe abstract relations in abstract terms.

Wundt's criteria of the two processes are as follows. (1)
There is a feeling of passivity accompanying the associative
connections, as opposed to a feeling of activity in apperceptive connections.[2] This gives us a distinct conscious
characteristic for extreme cases ; but, as we have seen, the
line between a feeling of passivity and a feeling of activity is

[1] *Logik*, I, p. 31.
[2] "Lectures," p. 312; *Phys. Psych.*, II, p. 476; *Logik*, I, p. 30.

not very sharp, so that the range of ambiguous processes is very large. (2) A second peculiarity of apperceptive connection is the greater unitariness of the resultant complex. "Every part of the resulting compound [associated] process is still independent, so that if it becomes dissociated from its companions, it continues unimpaired in consciousness. But with concept ideas, as with all conscious contents which belong to a logically coherent thought process, the case is very different. The significance of the individual is now entirely dependent upon the whole of which it forms a part."[1] The apperceptively united whole is also more definite and compact. The limits of the complex are more sharply drawn. There is seldom a limit to the number of elements which may unite in an association, either successive or simultaneous ; but the number of elements in apperceptive connection is always limited, and limited in terms of the unity of the whole.

A better idea of the relation between the two forms of connection may perhaps be obtained from an examination of the concrete processes included under the various heads. Apperceptive and associative synthesis, Wundt tells us,[2] are alike in the fact that the elements in both are lost in the unity of the whole. The alleged difference is that the apperceptive fusion develops from the agglutination. Now (1) the great dissimilarity in the nature of the instances cited renders it difficult for the reader to place the exact line of division between the total processes. A clang is given as an example of associative synthesis, and the formation of words from simpler forms is used as an instance of apperceptive synthesis. It is evident that the elements from which the two connections result are of an entirely disparate nature, and it might well be that the apparent differences in form of the resultant connection are mainly, if not entirely due, to the character of the components. Moreover, (2) the development from agglutination is a rather precarious criterion. The agglutination itself appears to be entirely distinct in its nature. The addition of the unity of rhythm to a series of separate sounds gives rise to a wholly new conscious fact. The compound word, however, does not offer so clear an instance of unity of whole as opposed to part. When, therefore, we ask for a direct means of tracing the agglutination to the synthesis, we receive no direct answer; nor do the instances given enable us to construct it for ourselves. (3) To the concept Wundt attributes another peculiar character-

---

[1] "Lectures," p. 311.
[2] *Logik*, I, pp. 13, 37.

istic, which distinguishes it from all other connections —
from the earlier apperceptive as well as from the associative.
This is the concept feeling, a feeling occasioned by the cloud
of dark ideas which surround the central or representative
idea.[1]   The 'dark ideas' are, mainly, partial judgments
into which the concept enters, and which in mass give a
peculiar feeling to the whole contents, though themselves not
distinctly present in the consciousness of the moment.

The result of a closer analysis, then, is to show that the
differences between the two classes of connection are less
striking than they at first appear.   Aside from the concept
feeling, which marks off one peculiar concrete form, but is
not very closely related to apperception as such, we are left
simply with the difference between passive and active apperception,—between the relative proportion of subjective and
objective determinants of connection.   As we have said
before, it is, so far as classification in terms of apperception
goes, a difference in degree and not in kind.

We believe that the above is an impartial and accurate
statement of Wundt's doctrine of apperception in its latest
form.   Care has been taken to select the salient passages
from his different expositions, and to work them up into a
connected whole.   It has seemed desirable to state the doctrine as clearly as possible, even at the expense of so much
space and at the risk of occasional repetitions: (1) because
the subject possesses great intrinsic difficulties, as is shown
by the frequency with which the theory has been misunder-
stood ; (2) because even the trained psychologist may be
confused by the conflicting views of other apperceptionists
(Kant, Herbart, etc.); and (3) because we have found it
necessary to make numerous references to Wundt in the
course of our own work which would not otherwise be intel-
ligible, unless, of course, the text itself were familiar to the
reader.   We also hope that the account given will fulfill our
original purpose, and be of independent value in itself.   The
special application of the apperception doctrine to the problems of attention, consciousness and voluntary action, that
completes Wundt's system in this regard, follows directly
from the essentials of the theory as here set forth : we have
given only so much as is applicable to our subsequent investigation.

The preceding *résumé* of Wundt's doctrine was written before
the appearance of his "Outlines of Psychology."[2] There is nothing
in the treatment of apperception in the newer work, however, that

---

[1] "Lectures," p. 311; *Phys. Psych.*, II, p. 477.
[2] Leipzig, 1897. Trans. by C. H. Judd.

differs in any essential respect from that in the earlier treatises. Some parts of the older exposition are omitted and others condensed, to adapt them to an introductory work, while yet others are given a fuller and clearer statement (*e. g.*, the doctrine of the feeling of activity, p. 189); but the theory itself stands as it did before.

CHAPTER III.

EXPERIMENTS.

SECTION 1. THE PROBLEM AND THE METHOD.

The purpose of our investigation was to obtain definite and, if possible, quantitative results as regards one feature of the phenomena of association and apperception—to determine the amount of change which might be made in an object ordinarily perceived or assimilated in a certain way without change in the character of the resultant perception or assimilation. The original impetus to it was given by the observation of some peculiar mistakes occurring in the experiences of every-day life. One of the first instances, and one which was typical of several that fell into the same class, consisted in the interpretation of the letters M A I L, roughly printed by hand, as a *number*. I was trying to find by its number (1423) a house which I had visited once before, but which had been so far forgotten that I could no longer be sure of it from general appearance alone. I noticed a house similar in aspect and situation to that sought, and went up to it. As I approached, I read the number 1427 on the mail box. I studied this a moment, and was so fully satisfied that I had been deceived by the general appearance that I turned and went back from the door. As I reached the street, I looked again at the house, which seemed strangely familiar, and then noticed the proper number, 1423, over the entrance. On looking again, I saw that the mail box was marked M A I L in rough letters.

Other mistakes of the same kind were made in different fields. I had myself, as I suppose most have, several times mistaken one man for another whom I strongly expected to see. Instances of striking errors in determining the nature of odors, while the subject was under the influence of strong suggestion, had also come under my notice. Many cases of similar nature are recorded in the literature. Wundt, *e. g.*, gives an example of the kind in his reading of the word TUCHHALLE, printed in gilt letters on a black ground. He could read it either correctly or as a mere jumble of letters, according as he expected the lettering to be gilt on black or black on gilt.[1]

---

[1] *Phil. Studien*, VIII, p. 337.

It is evident that in all these instances there are two influences at work. A group of immediate, peripherally excited sensations is supplemented or changed by certain other, centrally excited sensations. In Herbart's language, the apperceiving mass works a certain alteration in the apperceived elements. In Wundt's terminology, the new elements call up and simultaneously associate with certain old elements to form a resultant new idea. On either description the facts are the same : that, under certain conditions, a stimulus gives rise to an idea in some respects different from that which it would, of itself, usually and normally arouse. Our first aim, therefore, was to find a means of measuring the *amount of change* producible by the central supplementing. This must be a function of two factors : the intensity of the external stimulus which is at work, and the disposition of the mind at the moment, the mental " trend " at the time of its presentation. The stimulus intensity can be approximately measured, and the change noted which the corresponding sensation undergoes with change of that intensity. The mental disposition, on the other hand, lies far remote from direct measurement, but can, under certain conditions, be artificially varied. We can then measure the increase or decrease in the amount and kind of alteration which the sensation undergoes with each variation.

Numerous preliminary experiments, extending over half a year, were made in order to decide upon a form of stimulus which would be easily 'supplemented,' and at the same time be capable of regular and measurable change. We first tried pictures, colors and geometrical outlines ; but none of these gave satisfactory results. *Pictures* afford no adequate means of measuring the amount of the departure from the usual combinations ; they can hardly be broken up into separate units. Moreover, the perception of a picture is normally, in a greater or less degree, a case of associative completion ; so that it would be very difficult to ascertain the value of the difference between the amount of completion necessary when the part completed represented the object well or ill. *Colors*, on the other hand, are so simple that they cannot readily be 'completed ;' unless form is included, they carry with them very few natural suggestions of objects which they might represent. *Geometrical forms* themselves are open to both the above objections.

We finally settled upon the use of *typewritten words.* Although it is not entirely satisfactory to regard the letter as the unit from which the word is constructed, that assumption was, on the whole, the most satisfactory that could be thought of or experimentally obtained. Besides the advantage that a word may be roughly regarded as made up of letters as units, it carries with it as a whole a certain suggestion of what its parts shall be. The value of a letter may be expected to vary with its position in the word, with its form (long or short, round or square, usual or unusual), and with the smaller wholes (long between two shorts, etc.) of which it forms a part. All these variations, however, lend themselves to regulation, and in some degree to measurement.

At this point our problem divides, then, into two distinct problems. The first is to determine the variation in the value of the unit of stimulus under changing circumstances, *i. e.*, to determine the value of the *sensational* factors which are concerned in reading. The other, related to the former as end to means, is to test the conditions under which completion takes place; to learn the ways in which these conditions acted, and to discover, so far as possible, the relative value of each factor in the total experience.

I. The first part of the problem falls again into several minor problems. (1) The first which suggested itself was the determination of the value of each letter of the alphabet in calling up a word, and the opposition which its absence would offer to the proper completion of the whole. Some letters would have, presumably, more or stronger associations than others, and would consequently be more likely to reproduce the proper word, or to prevent its reproduction if they were misplaced or absent. Although our investigation extended over two full years, its results are too few to decide this point. They make it probable, however, that reproduction is very nearly a function of the ease with which we distinguish the various letters. The latter question has been carefully worked out by Professor Sanford.[1] The second part of Professor Sanford's problem, closely connected with the first,—the determination of the letters which are most easily confused with one another,—could also be solved in time by our method; but it was found more convenient for our immediate purpose to eliminate the errors resulting from these and similar factors by using the same words wherever the results of two series given under different conditions were compared.

(2) A second problem was to discover the value of the different positions of the letters in the word. It is evident at a glance that there will probably be some positions in a word where a change of the letters will be of more influence in preventing its correct completion than a change of the same letters in other positions. These have been worked out, and

---

[1] AM. JOUR. PSY., I, p. 403.

the relative values of the more important positions determined.

(3) Thirdly, our results throw light on the relative values of the different kinds of changes to which the letter may be subjected. We made use of three sorts of changes in the letters. We omitted the letter, substituted another for it, or printed an "x" over it to give a shapeless blur in place of the original. Our problem here was to discover the relative effect produced by omitting, substituting and blurring a letter. The last two of these methods were comparatively pure, but the first is complicated by the fact that omission not only removes one of the units, but also shortens the whole word, and brings other differently shaped units into juxtaposition.

(4) In a more general way we gathered information as regards the value of the length of the word in determining the character of its completion. This came mainly from scattered observations in the detailed records. At the same time, though we thus have indications of the importance of length, we cannot offer definite numerical results on the subject.

(5) It would have been interesting, further, to note the importance of the relative positions of the mutilations, where more than one were made, in determining the completion of the word which was shown. But as no more than two were used by us, except in eight instances, this problem also went beyond the scope of our work.

All of the points quoted may be decided by comparing the percentage of right and wrong cases, i. e., of cases in which the word is not completed with the cases in which it is completed. The percentages under two different conditions will give an approximate means of comparing the effects of those conditions.

II. Under the second general problem—the determination of the strength of the suggestion which causes us to overlook mistakes in the word—we again have several partial problems. (1) The first factor to measure is the effect of the word as a whole in suggesting what its parts shall be. We can here count the number of right and wrong cases which, under normal circumstances, appear with a given amount of change. Of course, we must take the length of the word into consideration, and ascertain how the strength of suggestion is related to it. In a first series of experiments, therefore, we must leave the other subjective or centrally excited conditions of perception entirely to chance, and make no attempt to learn the conscious disposition or trend,—only occasionally noting what the nature of these factors has been from the subject's report of his introspection. (2) In a second series we varied, and in a measure regulated, the more remote factors by calling a word associated with that to be shown immediately before this was itself given. The procedure introduced a new factor, which tended in some degree to create an artificial mental disposition, and the effect of this could be measured in the change produced in the number of words completed. We owe this method of varying disposition to Professor Münsterberg.[1] (3) We obtained some light on other points by classifying the effects of certain other factors which were brought out unexpectedly in the course of the experiments. The results are naturally much scattered, but are nevertheless, in certain cases, of even greater importance than the main line of investigation in making clear the efficiency of the different kinds of suggestion, and the nature of suggestion in general.

Our apparatus was similar to that employed, for another purpose, by Dr. E. W. Scripture.[2] It consisted in general of a lantern so arranged as to project an image upon a ground glass screen, with a delicate photographic shutter fixed in front of the lens to control the length of exposure. All the pieces were set up on a long, black table in a dark room.

In more detail: The lantern was of the ordinary type, provided with two double convex lenses. This was enclosed in a wooden case, with the necessary doors for adjusting the lamp and inserting slides, and an opening in front through which the cylindrical lens holder projected and which it fitted tightly. Immediately before the lens tube was placed the shutter, a Bausch & Lomb pneumatic photographic shutter. This was fitted into the front of a wooden box, which in turn was placed over the lens tube of the lantern, and supported by a standard. When all was ready for the experiment, and the doors closed, no light at all escaped from the lantern. A ground glass screen was securely screwed to the table 1.25 metres in front of the forward lens, and the subject was seated 2.50 metres in front of the screen, in a smaller dark chamber within the dark room. The words used were typewritten with extreme care,[3] then photographed and printed on lantern slides. When thrown upon the screen the small letters had a height of approximately 2.3 centimetres. Constant illumination was obtained, during the course of the investigation, by keeping the height of flame of oil lamp constant. Later experiments have shown that the arc lamp could be used to advantage in place of the oil lamp, but as the investigation was already under way before the arc light was in working order, the latter was not used. The method gave a

---

[1] *Beiträge*, IV, pp. 20 ff. These experiments, undertaken to prove the similarity between centrally and peripherally excited sensations, were suggested in turn by some observations and experiments by R. Avenarius (*Kritik der reinen Erfahrung*, II, pp. 472, f.) in connection with the effects of disposition upon perception.

[2] *Phil. Stud.*, VII.

[3] Typewritten, in order to secure greater equality of size for letters of different complexity than is afforded by print.

clear and constant image of the words shown, and permitted us to make a (for the subject) noiseless exposure of the word from the centre outward.

The investigation has continued over the greater part of three years. The preliminary experiments, referred to above, to discover a method were begun in the year '93–'94, and occupied about half of that year. Systematic work was begun with the chosen method in the fall term of 1894, and lasted through the year for the five subjects whose records serve as material for this report. Further experiments were made with three of the subjects during the year 1895–96. Professor Titchener (*T.*), Professor Margaret Washburn (*W.*), Dr. Alice J. Hamlin (*H.*), and Messrs. Cogswell (*C.*) and McVannel (*M.*) acted as subjects during the investigation. All but *C.* had had a good deal of previous training in psychological work, and were thus trained in introspection. Of these four, *T.* and *W.* knew the object of the experiments and had given advice in the preparation of the apparatus, material, etc. The other three subjects were completely ignorant of the purpose of the investigation. They were asked to read the words thrown upon the screen, and no suggestion was offered that would lead them to believe that the words were incorrectly spelled. None of them seems to have formed any very definite opinion as to the nature of the problem under consideration, and certainly none betrayed any strong suspicion that imperfect words were being displayed at any time during the experiment. We have made use of this difference in the attitude of the subjects towards the experiments in a later Section.

A few seconds before each experiment, warning was given to the subject by calling 'Ready!' and a faint diffused light was thrown on the screen, by slightly opening the back door of the box which enclosed the lantern. This was necessary, to give the subject opportunity to accommodate for the screen; it did not disturb the work. The door was then closed, and immediately after 'Now!' called, the bulb which released the shutter pressed, and the word exposed. Each experiment was recorded at length. The subject was questioned as to the general clearness of the word, and any peculiarity in it that he might have noticed, and a careful note was made of each answer, including any chance observation that threw light on introspection, disposition, etc. We asked the subject just what he was sure he 'saw' in every case, and encouraged him to mention any doubts he might have as to the presence of single letters, or a general lack of clearness of parts of the word. The close questioning (in which suggestion had to be avoided) rendered progress very slow, so that never more than twenty, and frequently not more than eight or ten words, could be shown in an hour. This fact accounts for the small number of experiments which are contained in the report, notwithstanding the long period over which the inquiry extended.

One of the first difficulties that arose was to obtain a length of exposure which would permit the subject to perceive the word without being unnecessarily long. It was found impossible to get any constant objective period of time which would be just long enough for the perception of the word and yet not long enough to allow the first perception to be corrected. The time lay somewhere in the neighborhood of .2 sec., but varied greatly with the mood of the subject and was influenced by other uncertain subjective conditions. The fluctuations were so numerous and so large that it was finally decided to give up constancy of the objective standard, and to assume as a criterion the subjective feeling of satisfaction that the word had been perceived. In accordance with this plan, if a word was not seen at the first exposure it was repeated, each time with a lengthened exposure, until recognition was certain. In the first experiments with each subject it was necessary to find empirically the limits of the time of easy recognition for the kind of words that was to be shown.

When the nature of our experiments is considered, it will be seen that this uncertainty of the time of exposure is not so grave a matter as might at first appear. Usually in psychological experimentation the object is to measure a psychical process in terms of physical units. Both psychical and physical conditions must therefore be considered, and as the physical values are more easily obtained and controlled, they are chosen to be kept constant. We, however, are concerned with psychical variations alone. It is a matter of indifference to us how the psychical condition is produced, provided that it is produced. We also had a direct and fairly accurate measure of the subjective state we desired. In this case, then, it is possible and more convenient to use the subjective standard and vary the objective conditions—the time of exposure —until they become satisfactory. The fact of perception is the subjective indication that the stimulus has reached a sufficient intensity. The chief source of error in this method is that the experimenter may easily go slightly beyond the point which corresponds to the minimal time necessary for completion. We could regulate accurately only the lower limen of perception, but the other was less accurately determinable. We had no strict measure of the point at which the original completion was overcome by the strength of the objective stimulus. The few changes of the first judgment, however, and the small number of cases of failure to complete that appear in the records of three of the subjects, indicate that the error was not very serious. And it was again possible to get a rough determination of the limit by the subject's 'feeling' that he had had more time than was needed. In that event the results were thrown out, whether good or bad. At most, then, our method introduces an error which is constant in direction, though, like all subjective errors, variable in amount. We may consequently assume that on the average it will result in a time a certain amount greater than the minimum desired, which will remain constant in all the series performed under similar conditions. We should expect from this simply a constantly greater number of correct readings in each series. As our results are entirely given in relative terms, an error entering equally into both sides of the ratio will not influence the final outcome in any appreciable way. Moreover, this error proved, so far as we could judge from the experiments, to be very much less than the chance subjective errors which would have entered if we had endeavored to make the objective conditions constant, and permitted the subjective to vary. Theoretically and practically, subjective constancy of time was more satisfactory than objective constancy. A steady increase in the number of right cases also proved very desirable; since otherwise we should have had practically no means of making comparative studies. The failures to complete would have been very few (especially with *H.*, *M.* and *C.*), if we could have reached exactly the proper degree of perception each time.

The actual times used varied between .1 sec. and .5 sec., though the latter exposure is but rarely recorded. By far the greater number of exposures were within a small fraction of .2 sec. Of course, any results from these data will be complicated by the fact that the shorter exposures were often repeated three or four times before perception took place, and often when the word had been completed in a wrong way, it was exposed again and another chance given for the correct completion. In such cases, however, one exposure proved to give but little aid to the succeeding, even when known, so that a number of successive exposures are not at all directly comparable with a single exposure of greater length. The relation between a number of short exposures and length of corresponding single exposure is too complex to be easily made out. Quite frequently, in fact usually, the subject did not suspect that it was the same word that was given in the series of exposures, so that there was no suggestion at all from one to the other.

SECTION 2.   PERIPHERAL FACTORS IN RECOGNITION.

(1)   We shall begin with the first problem upon the list, and seek to determine the relative *values of the three different kinds of misprint* in opposing the recognition of a word. It will be seen from Tables I, II and III that the several kinds of change stand in ease of recognition in the order: omitted, substituted, blurred. An omitted letter, that is, is most often noticed, a changed letter next most often, while a blur is most easily overlooked. This relation is what one would expect *a priori*. A blurred letter gives us in every case a nearly characterless impression, which has only itself to be supplemented

or completed. It carries with it almost no meaning of its own to offer resistance to the idea suggested by the remainder of the word. It is then only necessary for suggestion to work upon the single letter affected. The appearance of the remainder of the word is not in the least altered.

The relation between a letter substituted and a letter blurred on the one hand, and a letter omitted on the other, is not so obvious. It might seem at first sight that a letter omitted should offer less resistance to the completion of the word than a letter substituted. The greater effect of the former, as actually found, however, depends upon two factors : the length of the entire word is changed ; and, what is even more important, the position of the letters immediately surrounding the omission is changed in relation to the remainder of the word. In our experiments, that is, the letters on either side of the omitted letter were printed side by side without leaving an empty space. This, of course, altered the general appearance of the syllable in which the omission occurred, besides shortening the word as a whole. The substituted letter was on the same level as the blurred in this respect. It offered the outline of a letter, which had only to be changed under the influence of the suggestion from the remainder of the word. There is no alteration of the length or general form of the word, or of the relative position of the letters in the syllable immediately affected. At the same time the more definite outline of the letter which was substituted, as compared with the mere blurring of the letter, called up supplements of its own, which tended, in a certain measure, to inhibit the action of the suggestion. This effect is seen in the large increase in the number of changes recognized in the substituted as compared with the blurred letters.

We proceed to the discussion of the experimental results in detail:

TABLE I.

Effect of Different Kinds of Changes for Words with one Misprint.

SUBJECTS.	T.			W.			H.			C.—			M.—		
Kind of Disfigurement.	R.	W.	%	R.	W.	%	R.	W.	%	R.	W.	%	R.	W.	%
Blurred	22	25	47	23	44	34	8	49	14	3	23	14	1	20	5
Substituted	35	29	55	71	39	65	27	98	22	7	39	16	8	37	18
Omitted	16	5	76	28	9	76	18	32	36	8	12	40	7	18	28

3

TABLE II.

Effect of Different Kinds of Changes for Words with More than One Misprint, on the Basis of each *Misprint*.

SUBJECTS.		T.			W.			H.			C.—			M.—		
Kind of Disfigurement.		R.	W.	%	R.	W.	%	R.	W.	%	R.	W.	%	R.	W.	%
Blurred {	+	26	25	52	20	43	32	9	49	20	—	—	—	—	—	—
	—	47	16	74	24	43	36	12	65	14	—	67	0	2	53	4
Substituted {	+	10	8	54	29	15	66	11	27	29	—	—	—	—	—	—
	—	—	—	—	20	9	69	12	37	23	12	14	45	12	10	55
Omitted		—	—	—	—	—	—	—	—	—	—	—	—	—	—	—

TABLE III.

Same as preceding Table, except that each *Word* counts for One.

SUBJECTS.		T.			W.			H.			C.—			M.—		
Kind of Disfigurement.		R.	W.	%	R.	W.	%	R.	W.	%	R.	W.	%	R.	W.	%
Blurred {	+	21	2	91	13	13	50	12	19	35	—	—	—	—	—	—
	—	29	2	93	22	15	60	8	28	22	0	32	0	2	23	8
Substituted {	+	5	2	70	18	6	75	7	12	32	—	—	—	—	—	—
	—	—	—	—	12	4	75	8	15	35	7	11	39	7	7	50
Omitted		—	—	—	—	—	—	—	—	—	—	—	—	—	—	—

In the above Tables the results for each subject are found, in the three vertical columns, under the initial. The columns headed *R.* give the number of instances in which the misprint was noticed, those headed *W.* the number in which it was overlooked; while the last column shows the percentage of cases overlooked to cases recognised. The horizontal divisions correspond, as is clear from the Tables themselves, to the different kinds of changes. Since in Tables II and III experiments were lacking for *T.* under one head, none having been given him without association, it was necessary to keep the results under the two conditions separate. Consequently we have two horizontal columns for each kind of change. The upper one in every case is marked by a + sign to indicate that an associated word was called before each experiment, the lower one by a — sign to indicate that this condition of supplementing was lacking.

It has been necessary to give three Tables to represent the results upon this first point. The reason is that in some of the words shown more than one letter was altered, and it is not plain *a priori* what effect each disfigurement would have upon the recognition of the others where more than one are present. Table I gives the proportion of changes overlooked to changes noticed for each kind of disfigurement in the words in which only one letter was misprinted. Tables II and III give the same relations for the words in which more than one letter was altered. In Table II, the numbers stand in every case for the entire number of disfigurements, without reference to the question whether the others in the same word were recognised or overlooked. The misprint alone is considered, that is, without regard to its setting. If, for instance, there were two letters changed in the word, and one was seen while the other passed unnoticed, we should add one to the *R.* and one to the *W.* column. In Table III, the *word* took the place of each disfigurement, and when *anything* was found to be wrong with the word it was put into the *R.* column, no matter whether the other misprints escaped notice or not. It is thus possible to decide whether each disfigurement is as likely to be recognised when others are present in the same word as when it stands alone, or whether something will be observed to be wrong with the word as often when one letter is changed as when more than one are changed, or whether the percentage of recognitions lies somewhere between these two possible extremes. The interpretation of these results forms a problem by itself, and will be treated later. (See p. 351.)

In all the Tables, the results of *C.* and *M.* with association—where an associated word was called before the exposure—have been ' omitted. This is because the number of cases in which the misprint was recognised under these conditions was so small that the ratios practically became infinite. For *C.* we had 8 *R.* out of a total of 123; for *M.* 6, out of a total of 130. The omission is indicated by the insertion of a — sign after their initials.

(2) The second variation of the value of a letter as the unit from which we construct the word was connected with its *position* in the word. We have grouped our results to show the relative values of three positions: "first," "last" and "intermediate." The intermediate positions were again subdivided into "first" and "last," and each subdivision included one-half of the remaining letters when the word had an even number of letters. In the words of five and seven letters, the second and third letters were considered respectively, as belonging to the first half of the word; all others were counted with the last half. These two uneven divisions—of two and one, and two and three—which gave one letter too many to the first group in the words of five letters, and one too many to the last group in the words of seven letters, may be expected to offset each other in the total.

It will be seen from Table IV that for every subject but *C.* and *M.* there is a striking decrease in the percentage of recognitions as we proceed from the first letter to the last throughout the word. The difference is most obvious between the first letter and the others, and more between the last letter and the intermediate letters than between the two halves of the intermediate letters. And for *C.* and *M.* all these results hold except that for *C.* there is practically no difference between the divisions of the intermediate letters, and for *M.* no difference between the intermediate and the last letters. This seems to indicate a general tendency of the subject to *read through the word from left to right,* and thus to give the first letters of the word a more prominent part in the recognition of the word as a whole. Consequently a disfigurement of the first letter was easily recognised, since there was but slight expectation of the word that was to come. When, however, the disfigurements came later in the word the expectation was greater, and the error more likely to be overlooked. This, however, is not the only tendency which is active in recognition, as will be seen later. (See p. 352.)

Further evidence of the same tendency is offered by the fact that in the words with more than one letter changed, whenever one disfigurement was noticed, and the other left unnoticed, it was the first alteration that was noticed in the greater number of cases. See Table V. This would not be sufficient in itself to prove the point at issue, on account of the small number of cases ; but it adds to the evidence of the preceding Table. No other attempt was made to classify by position the errors in these words with more than one changed letter, because there were too few instances of each kind to give any satisfactory results on the problem. Moreover, the problem would be very much complicated by the effect of the different positions of the disfigurements relatively to each other. So that the question would require an investigation by itself, with more experiments than we could allow to it.

TABLE IV.

Effect of the Position of the Letters in the Words with One Misprint.

SUBJECTS.	T.			W.			H.			C.—			M—.		
Positions.	R.	W.	%	R.	W.	%	R.	W.	%	R.	W.	%	R.	W.	%
First	19	9	71	32	11	75	18	31	37	6	10	38	6	9	40
First half of Inter.	32	23	58	41	32	56.2	22	53	28	6	21	23	5	21	12
Second half of Inter.	15	16	48	39	31	55.7	11	55	17	5	24	18	3	26	13
Last	7	11	39	20	18	55	2	40	5	1	16	6	3	19	14

TABLE V.

Effect of the Position of the Letters in Words of More than One
Misprint.

SUBJECTS.	T.			W.			H.			C.—			M.—		
	R. W.	W. R.	$\frac{\%}{R. W}$	R. W.	W. R.	$\frac{\%}{R. W.}$	R. W.	W. R.	$\frac{\%}{R. W.}$	R. W.	W. R.	%	R. W.	W. R.	%
	16	14	53	20	9	69	11	7	61	3	1	75	1	1	50

In Table IV the vertical columns show the absolute number of
times in which the misprint was recognised (*R.*) and overlooked
(*W.*), and the percentage of recognitions. The horizontal columns
give these values for each of the positions in the word, for which
results were collected.

In Table V the first column gives the instances in which the first
of two alterations in a word was correctly recognised, the second
those in which the last was seen. The last column gives the percentage of the former kind to the whole.

(3) A third point of interest as regards the value of the
unit relates to the effect of the *addition of misprints within
the same word.* Do the misprints add themselves arith-
metically, or does some other relation obtain? It will be
seen, if we compare Tables I and II, after averaging the percentages with and without association in II, that there is
about as much chance of recognising a misprint when it
stands alone as when there are others in the same word. If
there is any difference it is *in favor of recognising a change
when others are present.* Thus for *W.* and *H.* there is practi-
cal equality between the conditions, while for *T., C.* and *M.*
the percentages are a little greater where more than one letter
was altered in the same word.

Our investigation, however, as has been noted above,
extends only to *two* misprints in a word. With more the
number would soon reach a maximum, beyond which even a
bare recognition of the word would no longer be possible, to
say nothing of recognition with complete ignorance of the
changes introduced. The other objects of our investigation
would not permit us to experiment on this point. For to
show any great number of words so completely transformed
as to make nonsense syllables of them would betray the purpose of the inquiry to the subject, and disturb the expectation or disposition with which he began an experimental
series.

These five Tables of results give us some idea of the conditions of recognition in general, and of the more important factors which determine that an impression shall be read as one

word rather than as another. Two factors in recognition are at once apparent from the results so far given : the *length* of the word, and the *position* and *character* of the separate letters. (1) That the length of the word is important is clearly shown by the frequency with which the *omission* of a letter was noticed. Further evidence on this point was given by such remarks of the subject during the experiment as that he saw only that it was a word of five letters, or that it would have been ' probable ' if it were not too short, etc. (2) The effectiveness of the position of the separate letters is shown by the increase in the number of times the misprint is overlooked for each successive letter as the word is read through from left to right. (3) Still another factor which is at work is the general appearance of the word as determined by the relative position of the *high* and *low* letters. This inference again is supported by the statements of the subjects during the experiments. In cases where no recognition took place, but some letters were seen, the subjects would frequently say that there was ' a high letter near the first,' or that 'it would have been [some word], except that I didn't see the high letter towards the end,' etc.

All these factors are at work at the same time in the perception of any word, and reinforce one another in accomplishing the final result. It is especially interesting to note the part played by the separate letters in recognition, in view of the fact that the reaction experiments of Professor Cattell and others show that the word as a whole is a unit, and separate letters require as much time for recognition as short words. This is a matter which must be discussed more fully in connection with the theoretical problems of a later Section. (See p. 373.)

SECTION 3.   CENTRAL FACTORS IN RECOGNITION.

In the previous Section we have considered the value of the letters, under different circumstances, upon the recognition of the word. In this Section we have to investigate the *subjective* conditions of this recognition, and determine so far as is possible their variation under different external circumstances. We have been assuming that the changes in the letters of the word offer opposition to its completion or recognition. We must now turn our attention to the forces which we have assumed to be opposed by these changes. These forces fall naturally into two distinct but somewhat closely related classes. (1) The first comes from the *effects of the word itself*, as a whole, *upon each separate letter*. This is the first stage beyond what we have called in the first two

Chapters the merely objective elements in or conditions of apperception. (2) Another and a more subjective class of forces at work are those that affect the general *disposition* of the mind at the time, the conscious trend of the moment. The elements of this second group lend themselves much less readily to experiment than those of the first, and are exceedingly variable and complex. We have, however, as will be seen in the latter part of this Section, succeeded in varying two of them experimentally and showing the effect of this variation upon the recognition of the word. As will be pointed out in greater detail when we come to treat the matter theoretically, we cannot entirely separate the two classes of conditions in practice. They are both at work at one and the same time, and the result is in every case a summation effect, from which we are not as yet able to learn definitely the exact part which each plays. We do, however, hope to show that certain special elements enter into this complex, and in a few instances to discover the effects of variations in the conditions.

(1) The main question under the first head is that of the effect of the *length of the word* upon the *strength of its suggestion.*[1] Does a long word give a stronger suggestion than a short word? or is there any other definite change in the amount of suggestion with, the length of the word? Our results prove conclusively that the strength of the suggestion which comes from the word itself is *entirely independent of the length of the word.* (See Table VI.) This result seems strange at first sight. One would certainly have expected *a priori* that an imperfection which affected one of five letters would be much more easily noticed than an imperfection of one letter in a word of eight. This apparent anomaly may be explained by assuming either that the strength of the suggestion afforded by a word is inversely proportional to the number of letters, or that the prominence of the misprint is, for some reason yet to be discovered, in no way increased by a decrease in the number of letters in the word. The former seems the more plausible explanation. It must be remembered that our results have shown that the *first letters* of the word are largely effective in determining the word which is suggested. We have also seen that the subject recognises the *approximate number* of

---

[1] The length of the word in this connection has a different function from what it had in the previous Section, because here we are dealing with the strength of the word suggested in determining the separate letters that come to consciousness,—there with the effectiveness of length and general form in deciding what word shall be originally suggested.

letters in the word before he makes out the word itself. It is evident, then, that if two or three letters are seen, their suggestion will be more definite for words of five letters than for words of eight. There will be fewer possible ways of completing the remaining three or two letters in the former case, than the remaining six or five letters in the latter. Consequently the strength of the suggestion will be greater. It must be admitted, however, that it is surprising that these two tendencies, apparently due to such different conditions, should balance each other so exactly as our results show that they do.

TABLE VI.

Effect of the Length of the Words upon Completion.

SUBJECTS.	T.			H.			W.			C.—			M.—		
No. of Letters in Word.	R.	W.	%	R.	W.	%	R.	W.	%	R.	W.	%	R.	W.	%
5	12	15	48	8	18	31	23	20	54	5	13	28	2	11	15
6	17	12	59	6	25	25	23	18	56	4	14	22	1	14	7
7	10	12	46	10	27	27	22	20	52	2	16	12	2	16	11
8	34	20	63	29	109	21	64	34	65[1]	7	28	20	11	25	28

In Table VI the figures in the first column indicate the number of letters in the words of the different groups; the figures in the column marked *R.* under the initial of each subject the number of times in which the misprint was noticed; those in the column marked *W.* the number of instances in which the misprint escaped notice, and those in the third column the percentage of *R.* to the entire number.

(2) Under the second class of influences, the more general factors which tend to produce completion and to direct its course, we shall probably find the effects of the entire conscious life of the individual. It is of course impossible to trace all the factors which are or have been at work in producing the general disposition of consciousness which determines how one shall read a word, or what effects the word shall produce, *i. e.*, what it shall mean for the subject. The more immediate influences are the *sensations* that come into play at the moment. These we endeavored to exclude as far as possible by experimenting in a dark room, where nothing could be distinguished except the light on the screen,

---

[1] The high value here is due to the fact that a larger percentage of the misprints were either of the first or last letter.

and that only during the experiment. It was, however, impracticable to avoid *questioning* and *directing* the subject during the investigation, and it was also necessary to use a faint light in *recording*, and in *adjusting* the shutter between the separate experiments. Another influence which it was also impossible to exclude was the effect of the *preceding words*. We shall be able to discover traces of all these effects in our experiments.

Besides the variable and uncontrolled factors, we were able to vary experimentally two conditions, and to study the effects of the variation in the increase or decrease of the percentage of errors recognised to errors overlooked. (*a*) The first of these artificial mental dispositions we obtained by Professor Münsterberg's method of calling out a word associated with the word to be shown immediately before the exposure was made. The subject then looked for the word under the suggestion of the associated word. This would evidently tend to alter the disposition of his mind for the moment. His knowledge that the word to be seen was associated with the word called would facilitate the entrance of the word suggested by the letters perceived. The striking effect of the association upon completion is shown in Table VII.

TABLE VII.

Comparative Results With and Without Association for Words with One Misprint.

	T.			W.			H.			C.			M.		
	R.	W.	%	R.	W.	%	R.	W.	%	R.	W.	%	R	W.	%
Without Assoc.	48	34	58	72	30	71	39	102	28	18	71	20	16	75	18
With Assoc.	25	25	50	60	58	51	14	77	15	6	56	10	0	89	0

TABLE VIII.

Same for Words with more than One Misprint.

	T.			W.			H.			C.			M.		
	R.	W.	%	R.	W.	%	R.	W.	%	R.	W.	%	R.	W.	%
Without A.	47	16	78	44	52	46	21	76	22	7	43	14	9	30	23
With A.	36	35	52	41	58	40	21	102	17	2	46	5	1	41	2

In Tables VII and VIII the first figure shows the results obtained
when an associated word was *not* called before the word was shown,
the second when such a word *was* called. The abbreviations are
the same here as in the preceding Tables.

In Table VIII the results for *T.*, *W.*, and *H.* are given on the basis
of the entire number of misprints, those for *C.* and *M.* on the basis
of the number of words, as the two Tables practically coincided.
(Cf. Tables II and III.)

For every subject, it will be seen, the proportion of misprints overlooked is greatly increased under the influence
of the association. There is little or no indication in the experience of the subject at the moment as to what the detailed
mechanics of this effect may be. In only a very few cases
did the word called suggest the word to be shown before the
latter was seen; and then the misprints were observed quite
as frequently as at other times. In most cases the relation

TABLE IX.

	Word Shown.	Word Called.	Word Expected.	Word Suggested.	Letters Seen.
H	fathex	son	....	weather	..........[1]
"	ovenage	mean	....	coward	c..........[2]
"	xrixoner	prison	....	dungeon	dungeon
	bauty	belle		buoy	b........y[2]
T	xrexkfaxt	morning	afternoon		(1) afrikant
"				acrostic	(2) akrostik
"				aggregate	(3) addregate
M	fashxon	style		author	author
"	escoxt	beau		arrow	..........[1]
"	favox	gratitude		harm	h(?)arm[4]
"	heavilo	lightly[5]		unlikely	..ik....ly
"	rtful	wily	....	steals	st....ls
"		ingenious	....	genius	g......s[3]
"		coquettish	girl	girlish	girlish
"		wily		sharp	sharp
"		ingenious	....	artful	artful
"	bauty	belle		girl	g....l
"	verbati	word for word	exactly	overexact	overexact
"	exxloxivx	gunpowder		magazine	maga(z)[6]ine
"	ramrob	gun		rifle	r..f..e
"	teochor	pupil		scholar	scholar
"	tlumder	lightning		illumine	..llumi..
"	winxow	pane		ache	aiche[7]
"	xover	lid		stove	stove

[1] The word was read definitely, but the subject could not remember what letters were seen.

[2] "Sure of the letters given, but can't remember what others
were seen in addition."

[3] Letters given are those which the subject saw most clearly. The
others were seen, but not so distinctly.

[4] "harm" was seen exactly, except that the bottom of the tall line
of the 'h' was lacking.

[5] 'Lightly' was understood as 'likely.'

[6] "The 'z' may be a 'g,' but I am sure it was magazine."

[7] The subject reported that he thought for the moment that *ache*
was spelled with an 'i.'

An 'x' in a word in this Table indicates a blur, *i. e.*, that an 'x'
was printed over the original letter.

between the two words was noted after the printed word was seen. In such cases the association helped the entrance of the word. It seemed to confirm the results of the visual impression, and to give a feeling of confidence that the word seen was the word intended.

In a few cases, again, it was found that the suggestion from the association was stronger than the visual impression in determining the word read. In such instances some association other than the one intended would be given in place of the word shown. They are collected in Table IX and given in detail to show the nature of the changes.

This is as far as the experiment or the subject's introspection will take us in determining the effect of the association. That the latter is not entirely introspectively reliable is evident from several instances in which the reader was positive that the association was of no effect, and in which the nature of the completion nevertheless seemed entirely determined by the association. The theoretical interpretation must go over to a later Section (pp. 374f.). (b) A second and even more constantly present element in these subjective factors, which affected the results of the experiments in a way that could be measured, was the *knowledge* which the subject had as to the actual purpose of the experiment. As has been said above (p. 344), T. and W. were working throughout with entire knowledge of the problem under investigation, and of the fact that the words contained misprints. H., C. and M. on the other hand knew nothing of the nature of the experiment, and every effort was made to lead them to suppose that they were merely to read a series of correctly printed words. Of course it was impossible to keep them in this state of ignorance throughout the entire two years during which the experiments lasted. No one of them, however, is definitely satisfied that he knows the exact purpose of the work ; but all have had attacks of more or less severe scepticism as to the correctness of the words shown. Of course, too, the mental disposition could not be kept constant for different experimental hours, or even for different parts of the same hour. If an error was recognised in several words in succession, the subject's faith would be disturbed for the time being, and he would be on the lookout for mistakes. On the other hand, if the errors had escaped his notice for some time, his suspicions would be lessened, and he would be less likely to observe an error.

The results indicate that the subjects were arranged in order of accuracy in distinguishing the misprints as W., T., H., C., M. (See Table VII.) In general this is the order of frequency with which they worked. Thus W. worked more frequently than T., H. than C. M., however, was experimented upon more often than C., though for a shorter period of time. It is obviously impossible to compare T. and W. in this respect with the others, who were working without knowledge.

It is evident at a glance that the mental attitude of an observer who knows that there are imperfections in the words is entirely different from that of one who does not. In the former case the attitude of the subject reached the stage of looking for mistakes which he expected to find in the words. This is really a suggestion antagonistic to the natural effect of the completion, and has a negative influence upon the normal tendency, as is shown quite vividly by the fact that mistakes were noticed in some of the correct words given as puzzle experiments in the early part of the investigation. Thus, of four correct words which were shown T., three were said to be incorrectly spelled, and W. either wrongly completed or made nonsense syllables of all that were shown. [1]

Here we see the nature of the suggestion entirely transformed, and intense enough to change the resulting perception against the natural tendency to completion. It is still a case of the effect of subjective factors, but of factors acting in a direction opposed to their ordinary course, as shown in the other subjects.

(3) Still other circumstances which were of influence upon the reading of the words entered almost as chance disturbances, regarded from the standpoint of the previous investigation, but nevertheless offer valuable evidence as to the influence of the more remote experiences in determining the nature and direction of the completion. While the two previous factors have shown themselves in an increase in the number of completions, these reveal themselves only in the nature of the completion. The former aided in seeing the word intended in spite of misprints and disfigurements; these become evident only in the appearance of a new word directly connected with a disturbance which has immediately preceded. Thus we find that many times a word is said to be read which is only slightly similar to the word intended, or is entirely different from it. Very often this misreading cannot be accounted for, and we must assume that its condition is to be found in some earlier event in the experience of the individual which has been overlooked by the experimenter, or is beyond the range of his observation. In some instances, however, these unusual

---

[1] For instance, T. read *FABRICATES* as without the *I, fraudulent* as lacking the *n* and *fictitious* as if it were *flictitious*. W. made FABRICATES *Sabrigates*, and *teachor* was said to be spelled *teader*.

changes could be traced to some incident in the immediate past.

(a) The first class to be noticed under this head is the effect of the preceding word. In our experiments we could not of course have each word stand alone; it must be in series with others; and one would expect, consequently, that the influence of the preceding words in the series would be shown in the nature of the completion. This was probably working at all times, but as we could not eliminate it experimentally and compare a series with preceding words with one without, we shall be confined to noting the influence (from the form of the misreading) in the few instances in which it became predominant and determining. That one single influence should ever have gained such an ascendency against so many powerful elements is an indication of its strength.

TABLE X.

Influence of the Preceding Word in the Series.

Subject.	Word Shown.	Preceding Word.	Word Read.	Letters Seen.
W.	fellw	Many adverbs in ' -ly '[1]	folly	folly
H.	ecently	(1) monopolict[2]	(1) metropolitan	m............
"	"	(2) "	(2) metropolitan	......p......
"	"	(3) "	(3) metropolitan	metro........
"	whenevxr	whatevea	whatever	whatever
"	stryight	kommonly[1]	straightly	straightly
M.	downwark	oulright	downright	downright

In Table X are collected the instances which come under this head. Here are included also two words which show the influence not merely of the immediately preceding word, but of the general character of all the preceding words, in the tendency to add '-ly,' or to read words as if they ended in ' y,' a tendency which was due to the large number of adverbs that had been shown by accident in the same series. In all these cases the influence of the preceding word was not conscious. The subject did not expect the word which deter-

[1] The first series, one of the longest, was composed of adverbs, many of which ended in ' ly.'
[2] Monopolict had been read cosmopolitan in this experiment, but not metropolitan. The strong expectation of metropolitan must have been from some union of the sensation with this completion after the experiment was over. The subject did not report any unusual expectation of the word.

mined the reading, nor have it clearly in mind at the time the word to be read was thrown upon the screen.

(*b*) In Table XI we have tabulated instances of the similar effect of some reading which was suggested when the word was shown more than once in succession. They illustrate

TABLE XI.

Effect of Previous Readings.

Subject.	Word Shown.	First Reading.	Letters Seen.	Second Reading.	Letters Seen.
W.	shabbilw	——	pl........y	shabbily	pshabbily
H.	recentlr	remember	re..........	remember[1]	rem.......
"	verbati	vorbald	vorbald	verbald	verbald
"	oulright	glacier	....	(1) alright	?alright
"	——	——	——	(2)	calright
"	cottrn	cottage	cotters	cottage	cottage
"	favnr	fervor	....	ferner	....
"	reglnent	negligent	....	....	regligent
"	downwark	downright	downright	....	downwirk
"	hixtoxy	beat		hiatory	

the gradual transformation of the first suggestion under the influence of the immediate visual sensations of the letters. At each successive reading some new element of the word on the screen usually asserts itself against the chance suggestion.

(*c*) A third influence, even more unexpected, was exerted by the word called aloud before the word to be read was shown. Although the subject knew that the word to be seen was to be associated with the word called, in five instances he saw the word itself, or parts of it, on the screen. That it should make itself felt against the positive knowledge that it was not to be present, and after long practice in experiments where it had been an association, serves as an excellent illustration of the effect of the preceding state of consciousness. Misreadings due to this influence have been brought together in Table XII.

(*d*) A fourth factor which appeared less frequently and was more remotely connected with the immediate experiments was shown by the influence of some word which the

---

[1] After re...... at first exposure had suggested remember from the fourth to the tenth exposures, parts of remember were seen which varied from rem to the entire word with the vague feeling that 'something was wrong somewhere.'

TABLE XII.

Direct Influence of the Word Called Aloud.

Subject.	Word Shown.	Word Called.	Word Read.	Letters Seen.
H.	greal	small	small	....mal....
"	aesidance	dwelling	dwelling	....welling
M.	hopoful	expectant	expectant	expe(c?)t..t
"	sihenca	quiet	obedient	obedien(t?)
"	sobsffance	accident	(1)————	auch
			(2)acquaintance	acqu......[1]

subject found it necessary to use, or was on the point of using just before the word was shown. It was impossible to prevent some conversation between the subject and the operator in connection with the experiments. Several times a further observation would suggest itself to the subject after the report on the experiment had been completed and the operator had begun preparation for the next experiment. Such remarks, or preparation for such remarks, proved to be disturbing factors. In two cases a word about to be uttered, and once a word that had just been spoken, was seen on the screen in the place of the word shown. (α) Thus 'somewhat' was read distinctly as 'moment' when the word came, as *H.*, the subject, was on the point of saying, ' Wait a moment! ' when the first signal was given, and changed her mind before the words were spoken. (β) Similarly the records of the same subject show that ' probabln ' was read ' possibility ' when the word was shown, just as the word ' possible ' came into her mind in another connection, and (γ) that ' hopoful ' was read ' because,' just after she had stopped talking in the midst of a sentence with the word ' because.'

The influences which have been indicated here are probably only a few of many which are constantly at work in determining the course of the completion and the word which is ultimately seen. Most of the others might have been found in the conditions of the subject's preceding experience. (ε) Two of these factors which come from an earlier time were occasionally shown in the effects which could be traced to the work of the preceding hour. When, for instance, *H.* came from a German recitation she would frequently give German words as readings of the word on the slide. *T.*, also, when called to the experiment from reading a French work,

---

[1] General appearance and length confirmed the impression.

would substitute French words, or words with a French ring, for the words actually seen.

A similar instance is offered by *II.*, who read 'onother' as 'oratorio' when she had attended a performance of 'Patience' the night before. Instances of this type are given in Table XIII.

TABLE XIII.

Misreadings Due to the Work of the Preceding Hour, etc.

Subject.	Word Shown.	Word Read.	Letters Seen.
H.	shredly	(1) sprach	sprach
"	"	(2) schrift	schrift
"	ouwards	(1) erwecken	........cken
"	"	(2) ————	......sching
"	shredly	wartete	wart......
"	shredly	schrecklich	schrecklich
T.[1]	ovenage	souvenage	souvenage

In all these Tables it will be noted that the subject distinguishes between reading the entire word and seeing certain letters of the word. Usually the word as a whole is given as read definitely and distinctly as a whole, and then several letters are given as most definite, or as most certainly seen, while the others are not so clear, or the subject may be in doubt whether they were seen at all. In many cases it was noticed that the letters which were most certain and of whose presence the subject is most confident were not on the slide, but were added subjectively. Occasionally no word is seen, but only detached letters or a nonsense syllable, which is made up partly of the word on the slide and partly of letters from the word whose presence is due to the disturbing influence. These facts show that for the individual the centrally excited sensations are just as truly real parts of the word perceived as the peripherally excited.

These questions of the subjective certainty of the correctness of the words read can be used still further to confirm many of the preceding results. So far, that is, we have been treating all kinds of completions and failures to complete as on the same level ; we have drawn no distinctions within the

---

[1] The instance mentioned in the text, in which the subject came directly from reading a work by MM. Binet and Féré. It shows the tendency to give a word similar to the French. Other instances of the same kind occurred during the same hours, but the records of them have unfortunately been lost.

two main classes. This was done for the sake of convenience, as they represent the general tendencies, and the
great majority of the instances belong to one division under
each, *i. e.*, the word is read as a word and errors noticed, or
the word is read immediately and the errors are entirely
overlooked.

Regarded from another standpoint nearly every word
given was completed. A word was read which was recognised as the word intended, but it was seen further that
something was wrong with some of the letters. Such
readings are, of course, to be distinguished from the few
instances in which the letters were seen, but no word
formed. In the latter case we may say that no completion or assimilation took place. Between the lowest form of
completion—in which no word is made—and the highest
form—recognition of the word intended without noticing the
changes—which we have given in the Tables under *W.*, there
are all degrees of completion. Thus a subject may recognise a
word and have a vague feeling that there is something
wrong somewhere ; he may recognise the word and know
the general part of the word which is disfigured ; he may
be mistaken as to the letter changed, or be right about the
letter changed and mistaken about the kind of change; and
finally he may complete the word without noticing that anything is wrong. Intermediate between the last two groups
there may be placed two more stages in which the misprint
is seen but is not believed or is believed to be subjective.
The two latter groups are placed under the general class of
completed words, since the final judgment of the subject
would have been that there were no errors in the word that
was shown him. All others were put together in the class
of words which were read as they stood.

The variations in the number of each degree under the
different experimental conditions are of interest as confirm-
ing the previous results. It will be noticed in Table XIV
that a greater number of words are not completed at all—
that is, read as nonsense syllables,—without association than
with, and more uncertain judgments are also given in the
former case. The cases in which a change was seen but not
believed to be real were somewhat greater in general when an
associated word was called before the word was shown,
though the difference is not so great or so constant as in the
preceding cases. This seems to confirm the statement of the
subject that one important influence of the association was
to increase the strength of his belief that the word read was
the word shown. The smaller difference where it was a
question of believing what was seen, not of being certain

4

TABLE XIV.
DEGREE OF COMPLETION.[1]

	T.		W.		H.		C.		M.	
	N.	A.	N.	A.	N.	A.	N.	A.	N.	A.
Completed, but changes noticed	68	40	57	60	60	14	17	7	14	2
Not completed	6	—	8	1	2	2	4	1	7	3
Completed, but noticed something wrong	4	3	12	5	3	1	—	—	2	—
Completed, but something wrong in the syllable	1	—	6	6	7	1	—	—	—	—
Completed, but mistaken in letter changed	—	1	4	1	—	—	1	—	—	—
Completed, but mistaken in kind of change	1	6	7	7	4	2	—	—	2	—
Completed, change not noticed	39	25	50	76	124	123	106	90	106	85
Completed, change noticed, but not believed	—	—	—	2	6	3	2	3	8	6
Completed, change noticed, but regarded as illusory	—	—	—	—	6	1	6	7	2	—
Partly completed	12	14	10	23	10	13	2	—	—	—

about it, was probably due to the fact that when the word
seen was in the proper class, *i. e.*, an association, one would
be more likely to doubt the letter demanded by the sensation
as against the letter required by the word read as a whole.
Another striking fact in this respect is the difference between
the subjects working with knowledge and those working
without. Subjects with knowledge, it will be seen, were very
much more likely to give a statement that ' something was
wrong, they didn't know exactly what,' or that ' something
was wrong in a given syllable,' and also to make more frequent mistakes as to the nature of the change, than subjects
without knowledge. On the other hand, subjects without
knowledge were much more likely to believe that the misprints were subjective, or that some mistake was made
about them than subjects with knowledge. This illustrates
and confirms our statements about the general disposition of
the subjects working under the two conditions. One who is
working with knowledge is practically looking for errors, and

---

[1] In Table XIV, the N. and A. at the heads of the alternate columns
indicate the results obtained without and with association respectively. The other symbols are familiar from the other tables and
the text.

consequently is prone to believe in the reality of every misprint, and to expect some to be present that are not seen,
while one working without knowledge expects the word to be
correct, and so is inclined to disbelieve that the errors seen
are real, and also to banish any indefinite doubts about the
correctness of single letters.

SECTION 3.   THEORETICAL INTERPRETATION OF RESULTS.

We have been assuming that there are two distinct kinds
of factors which influence the reading of the words shown
upon the screen, and which go to determine the nature of
the perceptions to which they give rise.   The first class
includes the letters actually seen upon the screen, the
external visual sensation of light and dark.   This we
have called the class of *objective* factors.   Those of the second class are due to the effects of previous experience, and
also play an important part in the perception.   These we
have designated the *subjective* factors, and have analysed out
some seven or eight of them from the entire complex.   We
have, now, (1) to explain and justify this classification of
factors, (2) to learn their nature, and (3) to determine
more nearly the part they play in the formation of the resultant perception, with special reference to the forms of
connection between them.   We must, that is, describe and
synthetise the factors which we have previously discovered
by analysis.

It is, of course, a matter of some difficulty to make out
just what happens when the word is perceived.   Introspection at the time of reading seems to be the only method
which can give us an accurate account of the process.   Our
subjects were encouraged, during the whole series of experiments, to tell exactly what occurred in the perception, and
were questioned on the general nature of the phenomena of
reading, so far as this could be done without invalidating the
results through suggestion.   The subjects were again asked,
in a general way, to give a description of the phenomena after
the experiments were finished.   By this method we obtained
a large number of coincident results from experienced observers under different conditions.   The subjects all agreed
in the following general description of the processes.   At
first, for a moment, nothing was seen but the light space
which surrounded the word, and a few indefinite letters scattered over it.   Suddenly these letters assumed the form of a
word and took on meaning.   This flash of recognition was
quite marked in all the observers, and was frequently made
manifest to the experimenter by a period of expectant silence,

followed by an exclamation before the report was made. The word seen seemed to the person introspecting to be accompanied by a rush of associations and connections,which aided in giving it a place in the whole of mental experience. Our present problem is to trace more definitely the different factors in this process, which we may call apperception, in the current use of the word, and to give its effects, conditions and degrees.

(1) Our classification of factors into *subjective* and *objective* was intended to set off, roughly, the *external* forces which are actively at work at the moment in producing the perception from the more truly *physiological* forces which are acting independently of any event in the outside world that is affecting the subject during the instant of perception, though for the purpose of our experiment they may be regarded as the stored-up results of preceding stimulations. From this point of view, the distinction may be regarded as merely relative. The ultimate source of both sets of factors is some event in the external world. They differ only as past differs from present experience. There is no absolute and ultimate difference in kind. All the subjective factors were once objective, and the objective in one experiment may become the subjective in the next. At the same time the distinction is real for psychology, because (*a*) at the moment the one is of a purely internal or physiological origin, while the other is produced by physiological *plus* physical conditions, and (*b*) the two give rise to definite psychological processes, which, as we shall see below, show characteristic differences which serve to indicate their separate origin. (*c*) Still another difference is that of the degree to which they may become conscious. The objective factors are most easily noticed when the perception takes place; while the subjective factors vary in this respect between the conscious experience which immediately precedes the perception, and which may return at the following instant, to the ingrained tendencies due to events so remote in time that they are now mere physiological capabilities, and could not possibly be remembered in their individuality; or, again, may be a part of the inherited nervous mechanism, and never have been in the consciousness of the individual. None of them need be in the consciousness of the individual at the time the word is read.[1]

The different subjective elements have been analysed out to a certain extent in the preceding discussion. We have been able to note the effects upon perception of the different

[1] *Cf.* Titchener's " Outline of Psychology," pp. 109 ff.

events which occur during the experimental hour, in the nature of the work just preceding, in the current affairs of life at the time, in the general directions given for the investigation and the knowledge of its purpose, and in other elements, which go to make up the individual character, but are too remote to admit of ready analysis or accurate reference to their source. As will be seen later, these influences do not all seem to be upon the same level, but are arranged in an ascending series, in which the higher controls and directs those below. While we have been using the event itself as the factor, we have done so only for convenience, and because that was the one concrete fact with which we could deal at first hand. Of course it is effective simply in so far as this previous experience has left behind it some permanent change in the nervous structure which is the immediate occasion of the phenomenon under consideration. The two classes of factors are the immediate conditions of the two forms of sensations or ideational elements of which all the more complex ideational processes are composed. These we may call with Külpe the peripherally and centrally excited sensations. They are the only conscious representatives of the two kinds of factors: one, the presentation, is due to the sense-stimulation of the moment; the other is the effect of the physiological conditions, which are in turn derived from events in the past experience of the individual. They are both definite psychological processes, correlated on the physical side with certain physiological processes. The distinction between subjective or objective factors and peripherally or centrally excited sensations should be carefully noted. The latter are something definite physiologically and psychologically, and originate from definite causes. The factors include all the causes of the perception, and very frequently can be known only by inference. In nearly every perception we find both subjective and objective sensations that owe their origin to the two most divergent classes of forces. The simple subjective sensation may also be derived from a number of subjective influences which are at work at the same time. The perception, then, is a very complex process, that can be regarded as the resultant of the stimulation of the moment and of all past experience; as the product of the reaction of character upon the present external forces.

(2) The centrally and peripherally excited sensations differ not only in the nature of the factors that produce them, but also very often show distinct attributive differences. Letters wrongly completed were said, e. g., to be of a different color from those which were actually present upon the screen; were less definite in outline; and were less stable, i. e., seemed to

be in motion over the word. The particular differences are shown in the accompanying Table (Table XV).

The relative fewness of these instances is to be explained from the fact that the subject is interested in the word as a whole, not in the details of the letters. We are dealing with a case of overlooking the letters under the influence of the meaning, as on p. 000 below.

378

TABLE XV.

A. Centrally Excited Sensation Faint.

Subj.	Word Shown.	Association.	Word Read.	Remarks.
W.	danxe	———	danger	" 'r' seemed faint."
H.	ramp	tetanus	cramp	" 'c' seemed faint."
"	dangwr	———	danger	" 'e' was dim or blotted."
"	verbati	———	verbatim	"Last two letters seemed a little dim."
M.	feathr	———	feather	" 'e' not distinct, but there was some small letter where it belonged."

B. Centrally Excited Sensation of Peculiar Form.

Subj.	Word Shown.	Association.	Word Read.	Remarks.
H.	hopefxl	despondent	" officion "	"Saw nothing until after the word was gone. Then seemed to see 'officion' in script of light letters against a dark background. Probably connected with after-image phenomena."
C.	shredly	cunningly	shewdly	" 'w' seemed to be only a blurred mark."
"	somemhat	slightly	somewhat	" 'w' seemed a little scratched."
"	quaintlo	picturesquely	quaintly	"Last letters seemed to be something inverted. The 'y' was not plain."
M.	ctaze	fad	crank	"Saw 'crank' spelled backwards."

C. Color of Centrally Excited Sensations.

Subj.	Word Shown.	Association.	Word Read.	Remarks.
H.	remotelk	distantly	faraway	"Expected 'far away,' and seemed to see it in dim reddish letters. The first letter was script."
"	camponiov	———	campnella	The letters seemed to stand out in terms of black and gray. Some of the gray letters were just as distinct as the black, but seemed less certain because not so black."

Besides the differences noted in the Tables there were two more general statements which relate to the nature of the characteristics that enable one to distinguish between the centrally and peripherally excited sensations, and which go to show that there is some noticeable difference between the two, but do not indicate definitely what the difference is. At one time *H.* was shown *January*, inverted by mistake, after *February* was called. The word was read *March* at once, and without hesitation. Immediately after, however, the subject added : "It was a dreary sort of thing, of whose existence I am uncertain." Again, the same subject read *recentlr* as *remember*, with the reservation that "something was wrong somewhere." Here the description was that "there were wheels of blackness going round." These come under very nearly the same class as the two instances in which the completed letters were seen to be in motion. These, too, both come from the records of *H.; gossi* was read *go . . . nt* with an *s o* which seemed to be dancing about in front of the glass. A more definite case of the same kind is found in the reading of the letters *chwter*, intended for *chapter*. The report in this case was that the letters *ca ? ter* were seen, and the doubtful letter seemed to be an *m* which moved about.

Few and scattered as these results are, they seem to show that the centrally excited sensation, no matter how certain of its existence we may be, possesses certain characteristic differences that distinguish it from the peripherally excited. It might be suspected that these phenomena were of *objective* origin, due to phosphenes, to eye movements, to imperfections in apparatus, etc. None of these explanations is probable, however. (1) The phenomena were of too infrequent occurrence, and (2) affected only the letters that were wrongly printed or were not printed at all. If they had been of objective origin, they would have been noticed much oftener, and would also have accompanied letters which were objectively correct. Nor (3) can the apparent motion of the letters be due to eye movements, since only a *part* of the letters were in motion, while the others remained fixed. Eye movements would have affected the whole word.

Professor Münsterberg[1] has argued from the fact that letters which are not in the word shown were mentioned by the subject as among those which were the most distinct in the word, that the centrally and peripherally excited sensations are identical in nature. This does not necessarily follow.

---

[1] Beiträge, IV, pp. 17 ff. Cf. Külpe, "Outlines of Psychology," pp. 183 ff.

The natural expectation of the subject is that any letter which is seen at all, has as distinct an outline as every other, and the ordinary quality; and this expectation is strengthened by the fact that it is realized in a long series of experiments. Then, too, with the exception of the first one, the letters are of comparatively slight value in reading the word. The word itself is the thing of chief interest, while the letters pass comparatively unnoticed. It might very well be that the letters reported as present were those central excitations that had attention called to them by some peculiarity which escaped notice later when the report was made. There is, at least, no connection between mentioning a letter as present and carefully noticing its appearance as compared with the others in presentation.

If it were possible to call the subject's attention to the letters without destroying the centrally excited sensation entirely by removing the suggestion that produced it, this method would, perhaps, furnish a means of making a comparison between the two kinds of sensations. They are brought under observation side by side, and the subject is almost entirely free from any errors of expectation. The great disadvantage is that which we have mentioned so frequently,—that the attention cannot be directed definitely to this point without betraying the nature of the investigation, and that the differences are consequently very likely to be wrongly reported or to escape observation. For this reason, among others, the method cannot be applied to make quantitative determinations.

(3) We have now to determine the way in which these different elements unite or work together to form the whole, the given unit of our experience,—in this case, the word. The concrete facts are that when a word is shown, it is either read correctly or some other word, more or less like that intended, is substituted for the presentation and given as if it were read. We have to explain why and how these letters or words are substituted. The first explanation that would have suggested itself to an old-school psychologist would have been that the substitution takes place by means of 'association by contiguity' between the *letters* that constitute the word. His explanation would have been in detail that certain letters on the screen are seen distinctly, and these call up and unite with themselves other letters that have previously been together with them in the same mental group. When the other letters that are on the screen, but not seen, are excited by this process, the word is read correctly; if the associations take a different course, another word is substituted for it. Now the tendency covered by this phrase is

certainly at work—no letters come up in mind that have not been 'contiguous' with the presented letters at some time— and is effective by itself in a certain number of cases. But it is no by means an adequate motive to the entire process. There is much that lies behind.

Each letter that is seen has a more or less stable connection with a number of other letters, possibly as many as twenty-five. The question immediately arises why one should be chosen in preference to all the rest. The answer that would have been given is that *frequency of connection* is the main determining factor. That it is one of the factors there can be no doubt. Our experiments furnish abundant evidence of the fact. In Table XVI are collected the instances in which the appearance of single letters in peculiar places within a word admits of no other explanation. The frequency of the instances in which the *th* combination is effective in this way is very striking. It will be noticed that *hereupon* is nearly always read *thereupon*, and *hereunto thereunto*, though there

TABLE XVI.

INFLUENCE OF ASSOCIATION BETWEEN LETTERS.

Subj.	Word Shown.	Association.	Word Read.	Remarks.
W.	hreunto	————	thereunto	
"	hreupon	————	thereupon	
"	erridateon	instruction	irridation	
"	horeunto	thereunto	whereunto	
"	hreupon	thereupon	thereupon	
"	ctaze	fad	staze	"It was for craze."
H.	remotelk	————	reac..tation	
"	henius	————	when?	
"	"	————	————	"There's a 'th,' somewhere."
"	"	————	....ture	
"	cottrn	————	cottra	
T.	remotelk	————	remotall	
"	mutright	————	intrident	
"	"	————	intrigant	
"	"	————	astright	
"	youthiul	————	pettijoy	} youthful was reversed on the slide
"	"	————	frittioy	} so that oy came last.
"	bxnker	————	walker	
"	henius	————	thebiles	
"	"	————	femulus	
"	"	————	Sphencius	"Sure of 'S.'"
"	"	————	...henius	"Something before the 'h.'"
"	cottrn	————	cottra	
"	gossi	————	gossal	
"	hreupon	————	threupon	"First 'e' gone."
C.	hreupon	————	thereupon	
M.	horeunto	————	thereunto	
"	shredly	————	shriedly	
"	sufdenly	————	suffently	
"	cottrn	————	cottra	
"	rtful	————	... th ..l	
"	disal	————	disable	
"	xeduxla	————	aedulla	
"	uvermore	————	evermore	"Seems to be an 'm' before it."

is no other reason, apparently, why one should be chosen
rather than the other. But it is not always this most usual
connection which is effective in producing the result. It is
again evident *a priori* that in many cases the frequency of
connection would favor several letters equally; whereas we
find that even then there is a definite choice made. Often
the influences that control this choice not only decide between
two 'associations' of equal strength, but overcome a
stronger in favor of a weaker 'association' between the elements of the perception, and may actually replace a peripherally by a centrally excited sensation. These cases are
much more frequent in our records than those which are due
to association of elements by contiguity, induced by mere frequency of connection.

We have now to investigate these more subjective factors
in an attempt to discover what the mechanism is that lies behind the selection. We find that it consists of an ascending
series of tendencies that work down through each other until
their effect is finally noticed in the control of the 'associations' between the letters. (1) The tendency that is most
immediately effective comes from the word as a whole. If *h* is
seen as the second letter in a word, it is associable with *s* or *t*,
among others, for the first letter. If the form of the word
and some other letter suggest that the word, as a whole, is
'should' rather than 'though,' the *sh* connection will be
effective, although the bond of union between *t* and *h* is
stronger in itself than that between *s* and *h*. In this way the
word has a retroactive effect upon the letters which might be
supposed to arouse it. It can replace certain presented letters by others that agree with the word, though they are not
on the screen, and place the latter on practically the same
plane for perception as the former. That the word is a real
factor is evidenced by the experience of the subject. No
matter how vague and fleeting the impression, numerous
words were read with more or less confidence in the accuracy
of the reading. The natural impulse was to find a word for
every group of letters, however indistinct it was. That is,
there was always a tendency to connect the separate impressions into something with a definite meaning for consciousness. We might offer further evidence for this influence of
the word in a fact noticed in the preceding Section, but there
not fully explained : the fact that the ease with which mistakes were recognized was practically independent of the
length of the word. We found, in that Section, two influences of the length of the word which are incompatible
on the ordinary theory of perception. (*a*) The length is a
very important element in determining what *word* shall be

read; so that a word would be rejected if its length did not agree with the length of the impression. But (*b*) the length had no influence at all upon the number of times misprints were overlooked, *i. e.*, upon reading the *letters*. These two different effects of the same attribute would be inconceivable if they were both directed upon the same part process. The contradiction disappears if we assume that the length in the first instance aids in calling up the word, while in the second we are dealing with the effect of the word as it works back upon the separate letters. This theory, too, admits the explanation there offered, viz., that the fact that ease of recognizing the misprints does not vary for words of different lengths is due to the opposed action of two factors, the increased prominence of the misprints in the short words and the greater strength of association between the word and the form and first letters in the shorter word. While the shortness of the word, that is, makes the fault more prominent, it at the same time strengthens the factors that tend to override and destroy it.

This fact will also remove another difficulty in the same Section. We found that the position of misprints had a marked influence upon the number of times they were noticed ; a disfigurement of the first letter was seen much more frequently than when it affected a letter that stood farther on in the word. This result seems to indicate that the word was read through to a certain extent letter by letter. At the same time investigations in reaction times have shown that a short word is read as quickly as a single letter. It is at once apparent, on our view, that the reaction time covers only the time required for the general form and length to arouse the word as a whole, and the misprints are overlooked or recognized during a more or less conscious reading—usually in memory—of the separate letters under the retroactive influence of the word.

Here the further question arises how we can explain this peculiar phenomenon that the word comes to consciousness before the separate letters, and is able to work upon them while they are being read. We have seen that the length and general appearance of the word played an important rôle in reading, while but a very few of the letters themselves were read at the first glance. This gives a clue to the puzzle. There is an association between the general form of the word and the word as a complex of motor, auditory and visual sensations in connection with other objects of perception. When the word is exposed, this association is effective at once and calls up a word without the least reference to the tendencies at work between the letters. It is the word that results from

this process which exercises supervision over the connection
between the letters.   There can be no doubt that the word
comes up as the result of the general impression from the
screen ; though it is again a fact that the bare association has
not such an important part to play as this bald statement
would imply.   For we have the old difficulty once more.   The
small part of the word really seen is associable with numerous complete words.   The principle of association is too general : it would explain too much.   We must look to more
definite conditions to explain why one word has the preference over numerous others that are on exactly the same foot-
ing so far as this one factor is concerned in the determination.   Here again, of course, the old-school psychologist
would have adduced mere frequency of repetition as the all-
sufficient explanation.   And it would have validity as a
statement of one of the conditions, but one of the less important.   Certain repeated mistakes that were made in reading the same word show that it is effective in some cases.   A
few words were misread once when shown on the screen, and
the same misreading was made one or more times in succeeding experiments, separated by intervals of several days.   It
is evidently an instance of association by frequency of connection between certain letters which were seen and the word
as a whole.   Practically the same sensation was received in
each case from the word shown, and the choice between the
numerous possible words was determined by previous experience.   In at least one case there were other factors, extraneous
to the form, which united with it.   E. g., the letters *ordnary*
were mounted in such a way that they appeared in one corner
of the oblong of light on the screen.   They were read *orchard*
several times at long intervals.   (See Table XVII.)   When
part of the opening on the slide was covered in such a way as
to bring the letters into the centre of the lighted space on
the screen, the usual position, the word was not recognized
during three exposures, and the subject seemed much confused.   But at the fourth trial it was misread in the same
way, with the remark that it had appeared in a different part
of the illuminated opening.   The instances of this kind are
collected in Table XVII.

(2) But besides the influence of the association, and of even
greater effectiveness than it, are certain more general factors
which   decide   between   the   various   most-frequently-con-
nected words that might be called up simply by virtue of
previous connections.   (*a*) First in this group stands the associated word that was called before the exposure was made.
This was active in two ways.   It gave greater certainty that
the word suggested should be the correct word, and thus

TABLE XVII.

REPEATED MISREADINGS.

Subj.	Word Shown.	Word Read.	Association.	Date.	Remarks.
W.	shredly	assuredly	——	Oct. 29, '94	
"	"	"	——	Nov. 5, "	
H.	imrovement	internal	——	Oct. 23, "	
"	"	"	——	Nov. 2, "	
"	ordnary	orchard	——	Oct. 27, "	Mounted in one corner of the space.
"	"	"	——	Oct. 30, "	Mounted in one corner of the space.
"	"	"	——	Nov. 7, "	Mounted in one corner of the space.
"	"	"	——	Nov. 10, "	Mounted in one corner of the space.
"	"	"	——	Dec. 15 "	Mounted in the centre, as were the others.
"	ordnary	ordinary	common	Feb. 23, '95	Mounted in the centre, as were the others.
"	verbati	vorbald	——	Nov. 8, '94	
"	"	"	——	Dec. 1, "	Remembered it had been given before.
"	monopolict	cosmopolitan	——	Oct. 23, "	
"	"	"	——	Dec. 15, "	

strengthened the effect of the word suggested upon the separate letters so that the misprints were overlooked more frequently, and it was also at times strong enough to supplant the word that would have been suggested by the general outline. (b) Other influences that acted in the same manner were derived from the preceding word, an earlier suggestion, and words that were called up in other connections. These have been fully described and discussed above in connection with the factors that aided in recognition (see pp. 358 ff.), and we need devote no more attention to them here. They all work upon the second association, that between the impression and the word, just as the word works upon the association between the letters, and it is only secondarily, through the mediation of the word, that their influence extends to the letters themselves.

(3) Nor is even this the end of our regress. The factors which determine what word shall be chosen may in turn be controlled by still more remote influences. These, of course,

may lie in circumstances remote enough to have lost their individuality in the general effect which we call 'character,'
or they may be effective in producing a more transient tendency.   Perhaps the best instance of the former case is seen
in the different reading of the word *escoxt* with the association
beau (bow) by a man and a woman.   The woman read
escort immediately, while the man read it *arrow* just as
definitely.   An example of the second kind is afforded by the
tendency to read the words as French or German immediately
after reading one of those languages.   This is not as good a
case as the former, because it is impossible to say whether
the disposition acted upon the association between the mere
letters, or upon that between general impression and word,
or upon the highest level of all.   The three lowest stages are
inevitable, and it is quite possible that in certain special
cases others of the same kind could be distinguished.   We
could find, that is, many more degrees in the increasing generality and abstractness of the factors which determine the
association that finally result in the complete perception.

Yet another factor whose position in the scheme is not
quite clear is the knowledge that the subjects possessed of
the nature of the experiments.   Its effect was probably due
to greater attention to the letters after the word had been
suggested.   It thus seems to belong outside of our general
scheme, and to be upon the same level as the word.   It
works, *i. e.*, directly upon the letters, and opposes the influence of the other more general factors which act upon these
only through the word.

In what precedes we have made the *word* the unit, the element of the whole perceptive process. Everything less general
leads up to the word, everything more general leads down to it ;
and it is itself the subjective factor which is of immediate influence in determining what letters shall be seen.   There are
now one or two other considerations which serve more fully
to justify and explain the important function which we have
attributed to it.

We have already proven that the word influences the individual letters, and is simultaneously effective with them in
producing the perception. But that is not all: for the word has
an effect on consciousness peculiar to itself and not due to the
individual letters of which it is composed.   As soon as the
word is presented the group seems to be known ; *i. e.*, in general, definite images tend to arise in the mind and form a
unitary complex within it.   The subject is reminded of something connected with the object which the word recalls, etc.
A group of related ideas is immediately aroused, and gives the

perception a setting in mind. By it we pass from the letters,
the single impressions, to something with a meaning for consciousness.   That it is the union with some other ideas, and
not the mere pronunciation of the word, or translation from
visual to tactual or auditory elements that is mainly effective
in recognition, is indicated by the fact that several times the
subjects would say, " I know what that is, but can't think of
it ;" they would have a 'feeling' that the word was known
before they knew what it was. The subject *T.* gave an excellent case of this kind,—which, however, started from the
spoken word called as an association,—together with a complete
analysis. The word *fireplace* was exposed under the suggestion
of *andiron*.   The word *andiron* was supplemented immediately by the visual picture of a fireplace, but no word came
to mind.   The letters *ace* were seen, and actually suggested
furnace before the rest of the word was seen to be ' fireplace.'   Here we see that the word was recognized, and gave
rise to associations before it was itself perceived.   Other in-

TABLE XVIII.

INSTANCES OF THE VANISHING OF LETTERS WHEN NOT APPERCEIVED.

	Word Shown.	Association.	Word Read.	Remarks.
W.	disal	———	deal	" There may be something between 'e ' and ' a,' but I am not sure."
"	braft	trade	art	" There seemed to be a queer letter be- fore it."
"	hxstoxy	English	atom	" 'Atom' was in the middle; I could re- member nothing else."
"	camponiov	———	campaniny	First statement was that the first was 'cam,' but after company had suggest- ed itself, said it was 'com.'
H.	brnefit	———	———	"All is confusion. Remember nothing."
"	foyever	———	forever	"There is a hair across the ' r.' "
T.	chimnxy	———	chimncy	"There are some crosses, but I can't re- member where they are."[1]
M.	nxious	———	———	"Letters were 'n l g g ful.' Can't remem- ber the order."
"	incetirity	———	———[2]	

[1] The subject made the further remark that he frequently caught himself making judgments in words to avoid trusting to memory.
[2] From the third to the seventh exposure vague letters were seen, but could not be remembered. At the seventh he said that he saw all the letters, but they disap- peared before he could connect them.

The instances given in this Table are some of the more striking examples of this tendency for the letters to vanish. It was noticed very frequently, besides, when words were not completed, but it seems unnecessary and undesirable to multiply instances.

stances were given in which the letters were all seen accurately, but it was not until some minutes afterwards that the word was read, i. e., aroused other associations which allotted it a place in the experience or knowledge of the individual. There is other evidence that this process of recognition, which we have analyzed into the origination of other associations, is an important if not an essential element in perception or assimilation. (a) Numerous instances show that unless the letters seen are fitted into some word, they almost invariably vanish. They cannot be remembered long enough to be repeated to the investigator a few moments after the experiment has been performed. That is to say, unless the individual letters give rise to a word, enter into connection with the rest of our experience, it is practically impossible to remember them. Instances of this kind are tabulated in Table XVIII. (b) Again, when the letters are recognized, the rush of recognition may be so violent that the letters themselves are entirely neglected,—forgotten, or not seen at all. We are interested only in the word which is the unit of experience, the smallest bit that can ordinarily find a place in our knowledge. When we get this we are so little concerned with the particular sensations that give rise to it that we pay no attention to them. They are not remembered as individuals. It is an association in which the original excitatory cause is not retained in consciousness, because it never really became a part of attentive consciousness. One link in the process of acquisition is simply omitted, so far as afterknowledge is concerned, or so far as knowledge is concerned at all, in the true sense of the word. The instances of this kind are tabulated in Table XIX. One of the best illustrations there is the overlooking of words printed in capitals. In the three instances mentioned it was known that the form of the letters was not seen at first, from the fact that it was seen later. Of the other eight times in which words printed in capitals were shown, only twice was it definitely stated that the word was printed in capitals. The inference is that the letters were unnoticed in the other six times.

This is essentially the same phenomenon that Helmholtz[1] called 'unconscious inference.' We cannot agree that it is inference; it is mere perception; and it also seems to be rather a perception based upon or originating from an unconscious, i. e., physiological source than an unconscious perception. It is evidently a process of the same nature as our space perception, as when, e. g., we get only visual images from tactual stimuli, and when the very complex per-

---

[1] *Physiologische Optik*, 2d ed., pp. 582 f.

TABLE XIX.

INSTANCES OF THE VANISHING OF LETTERS WITH APPERCEPTION.

Subjects.	Word Shown.	Association.	Word Read.	Letters Seen.
W.	biagust	abhorrence	disgust	........st[1]
"	whenewer	————	axiom	axiom[2]
"	henius	————	when	none
"	fathex	————	weather	"
T.	xnimate	————	animate	"
"	eaxth	————	earth	"
"	climxte	————	climate	"
"	forengn	————	foreign	"
"	Xebxary	————	Xebxary	"[3]
"	biagust	————	bicentiate	"
"	aprxcxt	————	apricot	————[4]
H.	iprecaton	vengeance	————	orence[5]
M.	aredibly	————	admiraty	ad(m?)iralty[6]
"	eaxth	heaven	earth	none
"	shabbilw	genteelly	shabbily	shabbily[7]
H.	ABOLITION	————	audition	————[8]
"	greal	————	greek	————[9]
"	FORESIGHT	————	foresight	————[10]

ception of distance is called up by retinal disparity or sensations from the ciliary muscle without any conscious sensation of what is known to be its occasion. It seems, then,

[1] .... st was seen at the first exposure, and nothing else, not even the general form of the word. The same reading was repeated four times in succession, and no more than one or two letters was seen at any time. It is given as a striking representative of the numerous times in which only a few letters were said to be seen, although the word was read as a whole. It is, of course, impossible to say how far the place of the letters was taken by the form of the word in these cases, and how far the letters seen were forgotten after they were seen, although probably both influences were at work.

[2] Whenever was also in mind after the reading.

[3] The word was seen some time before the crosses were noticed.

[4] This word was seen as a nonsense syllable at the first exposure; was correctly read at the second. The subject remarked that the letters were much clearer the first time than the second.

[5] Revenge was expected from the association, and the subject was so much surprised that it was not revenge, that she did not fit it into anything, and forgot what it was.

[6] First statement was that the word was admiralty without the " m," but before the report was finished " m " was said to have been seen. This is negative evidence that the subject is very uncertain about the separate letters that are seen.

[7] " Had a vague idea what word it was, and that it was the right word, some time before the word itself came."

[8] It was not noticed that the word was printed in capitals until the third reading, and then only the initial letter seemed to be capitalised.

[9] It began with a small capital.

[10] The capitals were not noticed until some moments after the word was read.

5

that we can have a sensation of so little interest in itself, and with associations of such great interest, that it comes to consciousness only in and through the complex process that it excites. (c) A third peculiar phenomenon in this connection was the tendency to recognize words falsely. Combinations of letters which contained centrally excited sensations were read off and pronounced as if the word really existed and was entirely familiar to the subject. Sometimes the recognition was complete and permanent, sometimes it was only a 'feeling' that the word was familiar ; sometimes, again, it extended to whole words, and sometimes only to certain letters or peculiar spellings of words. That is, two of the subjects would give nonsense syllables as good words, though they did not give any evidence that they knew what the word meant, or anything else in connection with it. The suggestion that real words were to be given was so strong that unfamiliar and impossible words were 'recognized' as real and familiar. It is hardly safe to draw any inferences from this bare fact, though it would seem to indicate that recognition was a definite process which could be set up by a habit, in this case the habit of reading words which

TABLE XX.

FALSE RECOGNITIONS.

Subject.	Word Shown.	Word Seen.	Remarks.
C.	caffea	caffea	"Is there such a word?" the subject said, and remarked a moment later, "Yes, I remember it now."
"	fellw	felly (felloe)	A moment later the subject remarked that felloe wasn't spelled with a 'y.'
"	kommonly	kommonly	It seemed all right at first, but later it struck him as queer that it should be spelled with 'k.'
M.	verbati	verbati	"I thought, at first, it was verbatum, then saw it was the plural."
"	kommonly	kommonly	Same phenomenon as with C above.
"	xexter	rexter	"I don't seem to be familar with that word."
"	window	aiehe	"I thought for a moment that ache was spelled with an 'i.'" (Read under association of pane. See Table IX.)
"	painxer	paintker (painter)	The first remark was that 't' and 'k' 'seemed a little run together,' and then it was added, "I thought for the moment that painter was spelled paintker."

could be recognized.[1]   Instances of this kind are given in Table XX.

Besides this complicated web of subjective forces which mutually affect each other and show their influence in the final perception, we must also consider the effect of the objective factors, the letters shown upon the screen, some of which have served as a starting point or foundation for this elaborate superstructure.   They are directly opposed to the former, and the result of the opposition is at times apparent in the perception.   We find in nearly every word that the correct reading of some letter is directly opposed to many, if not all, the subjective influences which are at work in perception.   Here, as in those cases in which continuous physical forces are opposed, we should expect that one would win, or that both would be evenly balanced, or that their resultant would be some effect related to both, but different from either.   We find the two former cases, not the last.   It will be seen in Table XXI that in some cases the doubtful letter is entirely unseen, while in nearly all other cases it is read correctly, or its place taken by a letter in agreement with the remainder of the letters in the word.

We also find results which could hardly proceed from continuous forces.   In some cases the two letters would alternate in consciousness.   First one would appear, and then the other,—as one force increased or diminished in strength. Again, in some cases both letters would be seen continuously ; so that the word contained an extra letter.   All these cases are taken from Table XXI, which summarizes the peculiarities due to this opposition.

TABLE XXI.

A. BOTH CENTRALLY AND PERIPHERALLY EXCITED SENSATION RETAINED.

Subject.	Word Shown.	Association.	Word Read.	Remarks.
M.	paInxer	....	paintker	See Table XX.
"	dangwr	fear	dangewr	
"	fxotbxll	baseball	football	There is also a " g " somewhere.
H.	fxotbxll	baseball	football	There is " z " extra somewhere.
"	kommonly	....	kcom....	
C.	quaIntlo		quaintley	
"	besIdn		besIden	

[1] Cf. Titchener, " An Outline of Psychology," §§ 70-72.

B. ALTERNATION BETWEEN CENTRAL AND PERIPHERAL SENSATION.

Subject.	Word Shown.	Association.	Word Read.	Remarks.
M.	hixtoxy	....	history	"The third letter alternated between 'a' and 's.'"
H.	dulpably	....	culpably	"The first letter alternated between 'd' and 'c.' Don't know which it was."
"	xexter	....	dexter	"The first letter seemed to be 'd,' 't,' 'i' and 'k,' one after the other. One letter seemed to be over the other and change into it."
"	redluze	....	recluse	"Seemed to be redluze at first, but when the word recluse came, the 'd' seemed to melt into 'c.' Probably 'c' and 'l' made the 'd.'"

C. BALANCE BETWEEN CENTRALLY AND PERIPHERALLY EXCITED SENSATIONS.

Subject.	Word Shown.	Association.	Word Read.	Remarks.
M.	kommonly	ordinarily	commonly	"But I can't make out the first letter."
"	fashxon	....	fashion	"Didn't see the 'i.'"
"	dulpably	guiltly	culpably	"'c' was not clear."
C.	soldoer	civillian	soldier	"The 'i' is not clear."

We must remember that in the greater number of cases in actual experience, all of these factors, which are present, are working together, coöperating to produce the general result. Thus in ordinary reading the words are *correctly* spelled, so that word idea and letters are at one, and associations with the preceding contents, together with the general trend of the meaning, both aid the visual form in calling up the proper words, and secondarily the proper letters.

We may now ask how the perception of the word is related to perception in general, *e. g.*, to the perception of a definite visual object. It seems quite easy to pass from one case to the other on *a priori* grounds, though we have not subjected the question to special investigation. In an object we have the general form, and a few details, in place of the outline of the word and certain of the letters. The total object takes the place of the word, and the other processes are the same as before. We have associations between the *separate parts*, under the domination of the unity of the object, which is itself determined by general experience. There is one function which the word still retains in perceiving a simple object; it gives *definiteness* to the perception, and connects with the remainder of consciousness.[1] What we have said previously of this function in the recognition of words is also true of it here for the finality of the verbal associate.

---

[1] *Cf.* Titchener, "Outline of Psychology," pp. 108 f.

SECTION 4.   GENERAL THEORY AND RETROSPECT.

We may now turn back to consider how our own formulation of this perceptive process differs from that given by Wundt and summarized in the first two Chapters.   The concrete process which most nearly resembles that investigated by us is *assimilation*, the second form of simultaneous association.   In the external description of the process we are in complete accord with Wundt[1]; but in the analysis of what lies behind the phenomena we differ from him very considerably.   Wundt reduces the process to an associative part-process of *identity* between the parts first seen and letters of the correct word, and an associative part-process of *contiguity* between these letters of the correct word and those usually combined with them to form the entire word.[2]   Apperception is present only in the passive form in which the objective or mechanical factors are alone determinant.   We, on the contrary, have reduced association to a very subordinate place, and find active apperception to be the truly controlling factor.

The first point to be justified is the omission of association by identity.   We are unable to ascribe to identity any conscious place in simultaneous association.   In successive association, as we have seen,[3] the identical element is the elementary process which acts as the hinge, the bond of union, between two total processes.   It is the unit that persists from one state of mind, and gathers about itself the new elements for another state of mind.   But we have in simultaneous association only what corresponds to a detached link from this chain.   How the element that forms the centre or core of this process comes into consciousness upon the reproductive side lies beyond the reach of introspection, so far as we have been able to apply it.   The part-process of identity may serve as a mental translation of cerebral mechanics; but it is not itself—at any rate, in the case of so habitual an assimilation as the reading of words—a conscious process.   Moreover, the identity process, whatever else it may be, is not of the same kind as the association by identity in the successive association.

Further: we have found in regard to association in general that it is but one of many factors in determining the word to be read.   Reduced to the mere contiguity of letter to letter within the word, to which Wundt ascribes such an important place, association is actually unimportant, though

---

[1] See pp. 332 f.

[2] *Bemerkungen zur Associationslehre*, *Phil. Stud.*, VII, pp. 340 f.

[3] See p. 333.

potentially all-important. It has been shown that only in a very few cases has this association been strong enough alone to determine what sensation shall appear, while usually it merely coöperates with other factors which tend in the same direction, and very often a strong association is overcome by a weaker, with which the other more general factors are in coöperation.

Far more important than the difference in regard to association, however, is that between the presence and absence of active apperception. We have but to compare our results with Wundt's description of the complex he designates 'apperception' to see how fully and completely they agree. (1) We noticed that the letters only become clear and distinct when the word comes, when they are read; previously they are vague, indefinite and uncertain. (2) At the same time the sense of relief is strongly apparent on reading. This is substantial evidence for the presence of previous strain sensations with their affective tone. And remarks of the subjects made during the experiments were in themselves sufficient evidence for the presence of both. (3) More generally, we have found that each perception or reading is conditioned in its nature by very much of the preceding experience of the subject; so that the process partakes of the very general character of apperception, that it tends to form a unit of the entering sensation and the remainder of our experience. Besides these most important attributes we have almost the complete list of minor accompanying phenomena. The word is preceded and accompanied by numerous more or less dark ideas, and the completion of the process is necessary for the words to be retained in memory. All the characteristics of apperception in its most developed form are present in the simple act of reading a word. There can, then, be no doubt of the essential identity between the group of phenomena we have been investigating and those to which Wundt gives the name of active apperception.

If, now, assimilation, the most important of the associative connections, is under the immediate control of active apperception, it is necessary to examine the other forms of associative and apperceptive connection with a view to determining the differences between them. This can best be accomplished by considering the concrete instances in the different classes. As instances of associative connection we have the fusion of tones in a clang, 'associative synthesis'; the reading of a word, 'assimilation'; and a space perception, the union of elements from different sense modalities, 'complication'. Subjective rhythm, the different stages in the formation of a compound word, and the concept, are given

as instances of apperceptive connection.[1] It is at once apparent that these two classes do not differ in any of the attributes characteristic of apperception.   One is not necessarily, or even usually, clearer, accompanied by more intense strain sensations, more easily retained in memory or more unitary in character than the other.   This first impression is confirmed by closer analysis.

For purposes of discussion all the forms can be reduced to two general classes. (1) Complications are practically assimilations in which the supplements come from a sense modality other than that which furnished the original peripherally excited sensations, as when a visual impression is supplemented by a tactual, to give the idea of an object. This sort of supplementing happens in practically every instance of perception.   In our own experiments we saw that the word was frequently a tactual idea, called up by and associated to a visual impression.   Assimilation and complication, then, can be considered as one, so far as apperception is concerned.   (2) We have already[2] ruled out the combination and transformation of words ('agglutination') on the ground of the complete dissimilarity of the material worked upon from that ordinarily present in the other groups.   The process, too, is entirely different.   The changes in language are due to slow growth during the history of the race, and only slightly, if at all, the work of any individual consciousness.   It does not seem safe to reason from these very general products of the mind to special processes, unless we can follow the connection in much greater detail than is possible at present.   So far as we can see, however, 'assimilation' would cover these cases also.—We have left, therefore, the clang as opposed to rhythm, and assimilation as opposed to the concept.   Now (3) clang and rhythm ('associative' and 'apperceptive synthesis') are evidently not on the same level. A clang is a mere abstraction, an element out of its setting.   We never find it in the concrete except as part of an assimilation, and it is only as the basis for the higher and more complete process that it has any real existence. The union between the tones themselves, is, probably, as entirely physical as that between the letters in the words that were used in our investigation.   They never come to consciousness without being supplemented and united with other elements ; they lie below the level upon which apperception is effective.   The connection, of course, can be regarded as 'associative,' but it never comes to consciousness until it

---

[1] Cf. Chapter II, §§ 1 and 2.
[2] P. 337.

reaches the higher stage. That it is, then, subject to apperception is shown by the facts connected with the hearing out
of overtones, etc. Rhythm, on the contrary, stands on the
higher level. It is a concrete process. Previous experience
has usually given us successive sounds and their concomitant movements in varying intensities. Consequently we
tend to hear all successions of sounds in some pattern, just
as we tend to see all groups of letters as words. And the
nature of the rhythm changes with the circumstances of the
moment and the previous history of the individual, just as the
changes in the letters are subject to these more general conditions. Wundt in this case, then, has been opposing an abstraction to a concrete process, or a subordinate constituent
of a conscious fact to a conscious fact itself. (4) The concept
and the assimilation are identical for psychology. We have in
the concept, according to Wundt, a definite idea, which can
change into and so represent any one of several ideas.[1] The
same is true of the word that was read from the screen. We
found numerous instances of the manner in which more or
less definite images grouped themselves about the word when
it was apperceived, and formed part of the whole of which
it was the core. That several different ideas in varied settings could and did come up is sufficient to characterize the
combination as a concept. The logical concept, i. e., differs
from the simple perception only in the fact that in the former
case emphasis is laid upon its value as a representative of
different objects rather than upon its psychological nature.
Nor can the often raised objection that the concept is more
general than the percept serve psychologically to differen-
tiate them in kind. When, for instance, the word ' horse '
is read and the reading is accompanied by ideas of horses at
different times and places, it is just as much a concept as if
the word is seen so imperfectly that no such associations are
found, and the general term ' word ' comes with the idea of
various more or less definite words in other settings. Both are
apperceptions; it is only that the control exerted by the general elements is more adequate in the former case than in the
latter.

Of concrete simultaneous connections we have now left but
one form, which includes all the others. And this is in
every case the effect of an external stimulus which arouses
numerous associates under the influence of external and internal conditions effective at the moment, and which may be
traced to past and present experience. The differences that
have given rise to Wundt's classification are not due in any

---

[1] Pp. 334 f.

degree to apperception, and several of them are foreign to the nature of the mental process as such.

The question of the relation between *successive* association and apperception is beyond the range of our experiments; but analogy and the experience of every-day life show that here, too, the differences either do not exist, or are not correlated with any differences in the amount or kind of apperception. It was pointed out in the course of our earlier discussion (Ch. II, § 1) that successive associations were but series of assimilations acting upon a central core retained from the preceding mental state. It is altogether probable, then, that apperception enters here as strongly as where the original impetus is given by an external stimulus, though the problem at present lies beyond the realm of experiment. We should expect that when the whole process is due to what we have called the subjective factors, the more general elements are more effectually operative than in perceptions of an external object: and introspection confirms this inference. It is also very evident that the course of connection between the different assimilations is controlled by the more general factors. This is confirmed by every-day observations. The course of a man's thought under given circumstances varies with his experience, recent and remote, his education and his character. Even in reveries and dreams we can trace the effects of surroundings and disposition.— Successive 'associative' connections, that is, almost certainly involve apperception.

The first of what are called the successive apperceptive connections is judgment. We must, however, agree with certain modern logicians that many of what are usually termed judgments are, psychologically, simultaneous, not successive processes.[1] It is fundamentally a mere concept. The exigencies of language alone are responsible for its apparent successiveness. When, e. g., I see from the window a man walking in a certain direction, the image of the man, together with the direction he is taking and the whole setting of the picture, brings up the idea of the University buildings. The process is as much one, psychologically, as the idea of a stable when the word horse is read. In order to convey this picture to others I must break up the whole in the statement, "That man is going toward the University." It is necessary to give each of the parts a separate word; and the fact that sounds must be successive is the only reason for separating the unitary complex in this way. To argue from this to the conclusion that the judg-

---

[1] Cf. B. Bosanquet, "Logic," I, pp. 80 f.; F. H. Bradley, "The Principles of Logic," p. 12; H. Lotze, "Logic," I, pp. 59 f.

ment is always a peculiar process, is to raise a defect of language to the plane of a psychological law. It would be going
beyond our brief, and also far beyond our powers, to develop
a complete and detailed psychology of logic. But the above
would indicate that the solution of the question lies in great
part in the necessities and limitations of expression, and in
the objective reference which logic must see in all mental processes. For psychology proper these differences do not hold.

While by far the greater number of our daily judgments are *not*
judgments at all, in any peculiar sense, but mere assimilations or
concepts, which take the form of judgment, there are at rare intervals processes in which active apperception is again at work upon
the developed concept, and forms from it a *successive* process under
the influence of the most general factors. This may be regarded
as the prototype of the abridged judgment we have been dis-
cussing. As applied to *real* judgment, the previous description
is, therefore, not quite correct. True, the succession does not lie
where the older psychologists and grammatical logicians put it,—
between subject and predicate; but the process is none the less a
process which is consummated in stages by succession. Cf. Wundt's
Logik, II, pp. 155 f.; Titchener's "Outline of Psychology," pp. 205 ff.

We are now in a position to formulate a scheme of psychology upon the side of intellect. (1) As the element of all
cognitive states stands the *sensation;* admittedly an abstraction from concrete reality. (2) Next in order comes the *idea*, a
compound or complex of sensations : this is also an abstraction.
(3) The simplest form of connection between ideas is that of
the *association*, which is, again, in no sense concrete. (4)
Above association stands *apperception ;*—yet another abstraction representing the influence of general experience in consciousness, just as association represents the influence of
particular idea upon particular idea. (5) The first concrete
conscious process, and the process from which all these forms
have been abstracted, is the *assimilation* or *perception*. This
includes Wundt's associative synthesis, assimilation and
complication, *i. e.*, all of his associative connections, as well
as the apperceptive connections of apperceptive synthesis,
the concept, the greater part of what are known as judgments, and probably agglutination also. (6) Beyond these
simultaneous processes we have the successive chain of assimilations, and (7), at the highest stage of all, the true
judgment.

All the concrete processes may be regarded as made up of
sensations and ideas connected and unified under the influence of the very complicated interaction between association
and apperception. Our answer to the problem of the relation between association and apperception, set in the introduction, is that both processes are artifacts, fictions, intro-

duced to explain the course of consciousness in the concrete ; that both are the results of inference ; and that association, in our sense of the term, is subordinate to apperception, and of far less importance than apperception for the production of any mental state. Although we have thus rejected for psychology many of the distinctions usually drawn between various forms of connection on the intellectual side of mind, we do not mean, however, thereby to recommend any change of the terms in current use. For pedagogical purposes, and to answer the needs of every-day life, distinctions within what we have called the assimilation or perception are very necessary. A perfectly good theory of the intellectual processes can be built up with association alone as *terminus technicus*, or with association and apperception together, provided only that the words are correctly interpreted. Our purpose is simply to insist on the one hand that conscious processes and their connections are not so simple as is usually supposed, and on the other that what are ordinarily known as the 'higher' and 'lower' processes are not different in psychological structure and mode of composition. Wundt's classification 'works,' and serves a useful end ; our one serious criticism upon it under this head, is that it is not intrinsically psychological, and that its logical basis ought therefore to be made explicit.

In the preceding discussion we have intentionally avoided the introduction of any controversial use of the 'unconscious,'[1] and of Meinong's doctrine of *'fundierte Inhälte.'*[2] It would be well worth while to work over the results of our inquiry from other standpoints than that actually adopted ; but the investigation would require far more space than is now at our disposal.

Mr. Stout's doctrine of apperception[3] is in many respects very like our own, and it may be well to indicate briefly the points of similarity and difference. Perception for Mr. Stout consists in the reception of a sensation into a 'system,' and apperception is the general term that covers the interaction between system and presentation or between two or more systems. The system, so far as it is conscious, is a unified group of sensations, and corresponds essentially to our 'perception' or 'assimilation.' We have no criticism to offer on the description of the effects and conditions of this complex process. The term 'system,' however, is also used by Mr. Stout to cover the *forces* which control the formation of the unitary group. The double use corresponds to the two meanings of apperception which we noted in the first Chapter of the present paper. The word is first applied to the force that directs perception, and then to the conscious product of this direction. 'Systems'

---

[1] Cf., *e. g.*, Külpe, "Outlines of Psychology," p. 291; Lipps, *Grundtatsachen des Seelenlebens*, pp. 125 ff.

[2] *Zeit. f. Psych. u. Physiol. d. Sinn.*, Bd. VI, pp. 340 ff. and 417 ff.

[3] "Analytic Psychology," Book II, Chaps. V-VIII.

are said to lie unconscious in the mind, and to receive and modify the presentation that finally enters into the 'system.' This apparent identification of result and condition seems to give rise to confusion in terminology, and tends to obscure the mechanism of the total process. It affords us no adequate idea of the play of forces involved. A second term could easily be found for the underlying dispositions which govern the formation of the conscious 'system' that would not carry with it any such doubtful implications. The remainder of the scheme of the intellectual processes is practically the same as our own so far as we can learn from a cursory examination, though the details are worked out much more fully.

There were a large number of misreadings of words during the experiments which could not be classified in any of the usual ways, and for which we could give no explanation. They must be regarded as due to events in the life of the subject that lay beyond the observation of the experimenter. It is, of course, not surprising that we were unable to trace *all* the forces at work, when we consider the comparatively short time that the subject was under observation, and how much of character is due to the experience in the remoter part. These cases are collected in Table XXII. They number (167) almost half of the entire number of misreadings. It may be well to compare them with the total number of experiments. We used 155 different words altogether, and made with these over 3,000 experiments. Not all, of course, gave definite results. Of the whole 3,000, 1,570 were either read as intended, or read correctly, so that they could be considered in the numerical Tables; and in 330 instances another word than that intended was substituted for the word shown. About eight per cent. of the entire number of readings, that is, were due to causes not given in the experiment itself, and to conditions that could not be traced by the experimenter.

The reader will doubtless find words in this Table which admit of an explanation that has escaped our own notice. We have thought it best to err, if at all, on the side of conservatism.

SUMMARY.

Our problem was to investigate the nature of certain compound processes which Wundt has classed under the two heads of *associative* and *apperceptive connections*. We analysed experimentally the psychological processes involved in the *reading of a word*, an *assimilation;* and compared the factors which we found operative in it with those that are present in the other forms of connection.

Our experimental method consisted in the presentation of words containing misprinted letters. The factors concerned in reading fall into two great groups, *subjective* and *objective*.

TABLE XXII.
Unclassified Misreadings.

Word Shown.	Association.	Word Read.	Word Shown.	Association.	Word Read.
W.			**M.**		
gossi	telltale	goose	favox	grattitude	harm
mcroscope	teloscope	horoscope	onother	the same	probable
eanth	sky	zenith	diapram	sketch	disprove
H.			disase	illness	death
rtful	ingenious	truthful	fellw	companion	friendship
manscript	book	narcotic	gossi	telltale	gross
forxibly	*vi et armis*	furiously	ovenage	mean	evening
aredibly	truthfully	reliably	biagust	loathing	bigamist
uvermore	eternity	unnecessary	foyever	eternal	evermore
———	———	emerging	hasitation	doubt	habitation
———	forever	everlasting	cxmmonly	usually	casually
chxmnxy	house	opening	forxibly	vigorously	formally
———	———	awning	somewhat	slightly	seemingly
reglnent	company	restaurant	regether	connected	regulated
Jxnxary	November	February	lrustily	confidently	restfully
Sextexbex	August	October	urgemtly	strongly	arrogantly
T.			downwark	upward	earthward
bossom	flower	bloom	xebxuary	January	Kalendar
latferly	lately	carefully	rxtixa	eye	spectacle
appxe	pear	spike	———	cornea	catina
C.			xeduxla	spinal cord	neurility
pxinter	artist	thinker	xcxter	paper	heresy
aemotely	distantly	velocity	hxsbxnd	father	bankrupt
lrustily	trustworthily	faithfully	chxmnxy	stone	church

W.		**C.**		**H.**	
Word Shown.	Word Read.	Word Shown.	Word Read.	Word Shown.	Word Read.
inxpedient	incandescent	clexer	clover	monopolict	osmopolitan
imrovement	increment	dexence	safe....	inwrdly	intensity
ecently	elegantly	onother	mother	cxmmonly	seasonly
cxmmonly	uncommonly	chwter	shutter	imrovement	informerly
aredibly	incredibly	cvory	envoy	ovtright	overhanging
forxibly	foreignly	———	ivory	kommonly	homology
latferly	jaggedly	diapram	decorum	nowudxys	hereunto
eath	sixth	cottrn	cottage	———	merchant
evory	sorry	besidn	lesson	———	towards
heroditary	heterodoxy	nxious	noxious	lrustily	legislative
xouxe	mouse	disase	dissect	uvermore	overseer
ramrob	raggot	cutom	outlook	vautious	virtual
hixtoxy	hickory	cotlego	cottage	wellnich	wellright
quxntxty	humility	wxnxer	tinker	mutright	nutrition
appxe	people	FABRICATE	refrigerator	neligence	intelligence
campaniov	astronomy	pertrtor	praetor	immensx	tincture
greal	real	redluze	realize	chwter	charter
M.		infxnitx	intermit	clixate	nitrite
aemotely	anomaly	ztubent	resident	braft	trait
inwrdly	warily	fellw	folly	immensx	locomotive
sidexise	sideways	———	jelly	ctaze	stagg
wbenevxr	whereupon	lrustily	density	evory	syrup
whatevea	whatsoever	mutright	sunlight	favnr	fervor
regether	regular	oulright	sunlight	heavilo	silver
kommonly	heavenly	vautious	various	eath	satin
oulright	allright	remotelk	remodeling	disal	dread
ordnary	scenery	bxnker	buckler	besidn	beautiful
xover	never	downwxrd	downright	reglnent	treatment
bxnker	barrier	**T.**		———	negligent
clexer	clear	monopolict	surplice	soldoer	sudden
dexcnce	defiance	forxibly	forkily	tomblo	trouble
favox	fever	downwark	dominant	xover	rover
ctaze	assize	shabbilw	ablish	eath	bath
cottrn	custard	mutright	intrigant	biagust	bigamist
heavilo	danville	somewhat	semblance	henius	helpful
rtful	restful	gratefal	accidental		
disal	disable	ramp	camp		
eath	earthen	grade	degraded		
grade	degrade	appxe	spoke		
fcllw	awfully	hopoful	chrystal		
ovenagc	outrage	tboxsxnd	inkstand		
foycver	whenever	clixate	climinate		
feathr	feature	heavilo	heavilie		
xouxe	azure				
xebxuary	auxiliary				
Scxtexbex	Shakespeare				
sendeuse	condense				
teachor	anchor				

The former make for completion of the letters seen, in accordance with the usual connection obtaining between letters, the nature of the word, and certain more general conditions of consciousness; the latter are derived from the letters themselves, and make for a literal reading. The following points were investigated :

I. Value of objective factors.
(1) The value of the letters as opposing or aiding the completion of the word varied :
(*a*) with their *position* in the word ;
(*b*) with the *character* of the letter.
(2) The effectiveness of the different kinds of change in a letter to prevent the completion of the word stood in the order: omitted, substituted, blurred.
(3) The length and form of the word tended to call up a word directly.
II. Analysis of subjective factors.—The subjective factors form an ascending series, from least to greatest generality, in which the higher work upon those next beneath.
We have :
(1) the association between letters in the word ;
(2) the word as a whole, derived by association from the fleeting general impression of length, form and the first letter, under the control of
(3) the more remote factors :
(*a*) an associated word called just before the word to be read was shown ;
(*b*) the preceding word in the series ;
(*c*) an earlier suggestion (this is valid only when several successive exposures were made);
(*d*) a word the subject had spoken or intended to speak immediately before the exposure ;
(*e*) interesting events of the preceding day ;
(*f*) the work of the preceding hour ;
(*g*) the general disposition of the subject, which determined the way in which a called word of ambiguous meaning was understood, and so its effect upon the reading of the word shown ; and
(*h*) the subject's knowledge that the words contained misprints.
III. Evidence of struggle between the two sets of factors was found :
(1) in the mutual cancellation of the different letters demanded by opposed factors ;
(2) in the alternation between two letters ; and
(3) in the persistence of both.

IV. Subjective and objective factors were found to possess characteristic attributive differences.

V. The word gave rise to certain peculiar effects upon consciousness.

(1) It fixed and made definite the letters, and seemed to connect them with the whole of consciousness;

(2) unless the letters were formed into a word, they could not be remembered; and

(3) in some cases, when the word was read, the letters were not perceived.

VI. Our general theoretical conclusion is that the same factors are involved in a great many of the forms of intellectual connection usually distinguished by psychologists; and that if the classificatory schemes in current use are to be retained, their retention must be justified on other than psychological grounds.[1]

---

[1] We are now engaged upon an analysis of the psychology involved in the modern logic from the standpoint of this investigation.